*Always from Somewhere Else*

# Always from Somewhere Else

## A MEMOIR OF MY CHILEAN JEWISH FATHER

### MARJORIE AGOSÍN

TRANSLATED FROM THE SPANISH
BY CELESTE KOSTOPULOS-COOPERMAN

INTRODUCTION BY ELIZABETH ROSA HORAN

THE FEMINIST PRESS AT THE CITY UNIVERSITY OF NEW YORK
NEW YORK

Published by
The Feminist Press at The City University of New York
Wingate Hall, City College
Convent Avenue at 138th Street
New York, NY 10031

First edition, 1998

Library of Congress Cataloging-in-Publication Data
Agosín, Marjorie.
    Always from somewhere else : a memoir of my Chilean Jewish father / Marjorie
       Agosín ; translated from the Spanish by Celeste Kostopulos-Cooperman ;
       introduction by Elizabeth Rosa Horan. – 1st ed.
       p.  cm. – (The Helen Rose Scheuer Jewish women's series)
    ISBN 1-55861-195-9 (alk. paper)
    I. Agosín, Moises, 1923– . II. Jews–Chile–Biography. III. Chile–Biography. IV.
       Kostopulos-Cooperman, Celeste.
F3285.J4A35   1998
983/.004924/0092 b 21                                  98-036346
                                                          CIP

Steven H. Scheuer, in memory of his mother and in celebration of her life and the 100th anniversary of her birth (1995), has been pleased to endow the Helen Rose Scheuer Jewish Women's Series. *Always from Somewhere Else* is the fifth named book in the series.

Text design by Dayna Navaro
Printed on acid-free paper by R.R. Donnelley & Sons Company
Manufactured in the United States of America.

# CONTENTS

# ACKNOWLEDGMENTS

I want to thank the people who have participated with me in the making and remaking of *Always from Somewhere Else.*

My father, Moisés Agosín, is one of the most private people I have ever known. Nevertheless, in a spirit of great generosity and love, he decided to tell me his story.

My mother, Frida Halpern Agosín, gave me her time and her loving attention and filled in so many spaces and secrets.

My translator, Celeste Kostopulos-Cooperman, took great care in giving my work an authentic and poignant voice in English. Elizabeth Rosa Horan provided wonderful context and insights. I am grateful to both of them.

At The Feminist Press, my editor, Jean Casella, worked magic on my text, arranging and rearranging sections and making sure that the ideas and the language would flow. I am a most fortunate poet to have had the opportunity to work with her, and I thank her for her sensitivity. I also thank publisher Florence Howe, who gave my book a welcoming home, and publicists Jennifer Dorr and Gloria Weiner, who are already working to bring it an audience.

I want to acknowledge the presence of Alida Brill and Steven Scheuer in my life and in the writing of this book. I am joyful that my books have become part of the Helen

Rose Scheuer Jewish Women's series and that they honor the memory of Steven's mother as well as my own ancestors. Alida and Steven's love and belief in my work have been unsurpassed, and I am deeply grateful for their support.

Finally, I want to thank my two children, Joseph and Sonia, who have encouraged me to write about their yeyo, their grandfather, and who are captivated by his eccentricities and his tenderness. I know that he—and I—will live happily in the memories of their future days.

*Always from Somewhere Else* is dedicated to my father, for his gentleness and his unparalleled dignity, for his silences and his eloquent visions, and most of all for his love and the tenacity of his hope.

I dedicate it, as well, to all of us who inhabit and share this earth: we are all uncertain travellers, strangers among friends, friends among strangers.

Marjorie Agosín<br>
Wellesley, Massachusetts<br>
June 1998

## TRANSLATOR'S ACKNOWLEDGMENTS

Every translator needs the assistance of readers with a sharp critical eye and with the perspicacity to identify deviations in the otherwise seamless landscape of the written word. I would like to thank, in particular, my friends and colleagues, Carol Dine and Jeclyn Medoff, for their careful reading of the manuscript and their insightful commentaries and suggestions. They helped me sharpen my linguistic tools and make this memoir as powerful in English as it is in Spanish.

Celeste Kostopulos-Cooperman
Boston
June 1998

# INTRODUCTION
## Reading the Book of Memory:
## Moisés and Marjorie Agosín

### I. THE ROMANCE OF ORIGINS

#### FROM SOUTHERN RUSSIA TO WESTERN CHILE

A range of histories and places converges in this book of remembrance. The recollections of the doctor, scientist, and classical pianist Moisés Agosín, filtered through the meditative attention of his daughter, the poet Marjorie Agosín, span a century of migrations. The search for origins goes back to Sebastopol, to 1890, to the daily round of Raquel, the music-lover and cigarette-maker, and Abraham, the literate, secular apprentice to his tailor uncles. Their early life together offers a synopsis of the turn away from village to city life, ranging across residences in a series of tumbledown ports. They meet and their oldest son is born in Odessa, the unabashedly newest, least Russian city of the Tzar, a place almost without a history, sprung up in the mid-nineteenth century, which Mark Twain visited and proclaimed nouveau riche—that is, American.

The Odessa of Marjorie Agosín's grandparents Abraham and Raquel might have promised, in 1910, a temporary haven, a respite from the bloody Crimea and murderous pogroms. But by 1917 Russia to the north and east and Europe to the west had been swept up in war. We should not forget or underestimate the magnitude of that war, which brought down empires, destroyed human life on a theretofore unknown scale, and left Central Europe in ruins. Abraham, one of the lucky ones, finds his way back from the trenches, crossing mountain snow and muddy plains. Among the masses of young men drafted to fight with no compensation to support the interests of competing and insatiable monarchs, capitalists, and ideologues, he returns unmaimed and with a clear sense that his own survival, and his family's, lies elsewhere. Their flight to Byzantium—which is, despite all its minarets, identified with the West—offers some years of sanity and as much safety as poverty will allow. The port of Istanbul is a stopping place, a strip of land at the edge of the sea where travelers descending from mountains or trudging across plains meet and climb onto boats, even as an earlier set of passengers clambers off.

Exchanging one port for another, Abraham the tailor from Sebastopol, former draftee into the armies of the Tzar, embraces with his family a progressively international identity. By the time his youngest son, Moisés, is born in Marseilles, the Eastern European world that he and his wife Raquel knew as children and adolescents is in modern terms centuries away. Perched on the underbelly of France, Marseilles is and was resolutely Mediterranean, scouted by Phoenician sailors, colonized by Greek traders, administered by Roman bureaucrats, decimated by Crusades, and now populated by refugees and immigrants from former French North

Africa. Rather than hovering on the crumbling edges of two once-proud empires, Tzarist Russia and Austria-Hungary, Abraham and his family close their eyes and leap into one of the newer parts of the New World.

If Odessa and Istanbul stand for the nineteenth century coming to a close, then Marseilles and the difficult decision to move to Chile stands for a flight into the twentieth century, undertaken with the awareness that this will be a fully Western world. Abraham and Raquel seem to have learned by 1923 to put aside the past and imagine a future in which the map of central Chile would be superimposed on that of Central and Eastern Europe. For their grandchildren, the map of Chile and Latin America would be continuously juxtaposed to that of the United States and Europe. Like Odessa or Istanbul, like Vienna or Marseilles, Valparaíso, chaotic and chancy, the newest of the new, offers just the place for transformation for European immigrants who, in coming to Chile prior to the 1924 opening of the Panama Canal, were literally and figuratively navigating by the stars, rounding the Horn or crossing the Andes into another world. Despite its earthquakes, treacherous winds, and remoteness from other large ports, nineteenth-century Valparaíso was one of the busiest ports on the Pacific, bringing fortune hunters around the Horn to the gold fields of California, picking up cargo bound for the western coasts of the United States, Canada, and Latin America, and serving as a center for Chilean expansion to the north. In the late nineteenth century, Valparaíso in particular felt the influence of the British, above all in habits that touched on commerce. While the navy has had a strong British influence, Chile's army traditions are largely derived from Prussia.

European influence in Chile was and is a remarkable aspect of the development of the national mythology, which among other things holds that Chileans are extremely hospitable to foreigners. It is a myth I can corroborate while pointing out that such openness occurs only after the guest has been lured into the overlapping grids of ethnicity, nationality, and religion by way of gentle inquiries as to where one was born, raised, and—above all, without fail but nervously—the questions, "Where is your surname from? What is your blood?" with the minimally accurate answer (for example, "Ireland") producing in the interrogator a palpable relief and sense of confirmation. *Always from Somewhere Else* addresses the unspoken anxiety behind the national myth of "European" Chile, in which the welcome foreigner will be well-to-do, Western European, preferably Catholic or tolerably Christian. Regardless of national origin, the Jew is set apart. Such pride in "European" origins underscores the perfidious acceptability of the marriage of gentility, nationalism, and anti-Semitism in Chile—as in Germany, England, or the United States—before and after the Holocaust.

In the pre-Holocaust world between the wars, the formerly Russian Abraham and Raquel stand in stark contrast to their origins-obsessed neighbors, casting aside residences and languages like so much improvised furniture. With their army of growing sons they hop from one boat to the next, crossing thresholds, making do, living in purely temporary quarters, using a door for a table and living squashed into tenements and near cemeteries with emigrants like and unlike themselves, until they reach Quillota, their last stop, with its score of churches for some twenty thousand inhabitants. While Raquel on occasion might draw the curtains on all three floors of her house to light the Shabbat candles, Abraham leaves off attending synagogue (if ever he had been in the habit of doing so): he and his sons are following Abraham's older brother Marcos, observant Freemason and secret Jew. The broader the expanse of sea separating the Agosíns from the past, the more the four brothers reach for a level of assimilation that Chile, for all its vaunted tradition of hospitality to foreigners, ultimately withholds.

What is Russia to a Jew born in Sebastopol, raised in Odessa, settled in Chile, conversant with Syrians and Turks? Being Jewish in Russia robbed Abraham of a childhood playing chess and marbles, forcing him from age eight to learn and practice the useful trade of tailor. What does Russia, abandoned three moves earlier, matter to a tailor who knows above all to take the measure of means, and in so doing sleeps where he may, with his wife resolving that their children, in Chile, will speak Spanish. Being Jewish in Chile keeps his children out of private schools. Only the youngest, the determined

Moisés, aims for a profession beyond the few allowed to Jews. Abraham is among the few successfully secular citizens of a nation that attends more faithfully to the construction and upkeep of its churches than to its public schools or hospitals. This grandfather is nonetheless a "faithful follower of his people's tradition," performing acts of charity towards the nearby poor, nuns, and students, rather than the far-away synagogue.

From the beginning of the twentieth century, Russia has attracted the interest of Chileans, even or perhaps especially in the provinces. In 1906, that is, prior to the advent of Bolshevism, the young Lucila Godoy Alcayaga, who later became the Nobel Laureate Gabriela Mistral, wrote approvingly in provincial newspapers of the example of Russia in shrugging off feudalism and moving forward. Such demonstrations of international interest brought real risks, in her case attracting the attention of a local priest, who rewarded her publications by excluding her from the local schools. Interest in Russia as a similarly agricultural, feudal land attempting to move into the twentieth century was typical among many Chileans and other Latin Americans in the years leading up to the mid-twentieth century: for Chilean writers such as Teitelboim and Neruda, for César Vallejo of Peru, for Carmen Lyra in Costa Rica, the condition of Russia stood as an analogy to the peripheral, agrarian isolation, wild mountains, and rapidly industrializing cities of the New World. It is Abraham's peculiar fate that Russia returns, even as he moves from it, physically and temporally—that the fearful year prior to his death is over-shadowed by the certainty of a military coup support-ed by Chileans who regard Marxism, psychoanalysis, and Western feminism as foreign contaminants, who burn books as temporary substitute for the burning of people as heretics, non-conformists.

Abraham aimed high but lost much. His losses began long before he became an exile. They began in Russia, which made him one of those "forgotten men," ex-soldiers, survivors of war who, like my own grand-father, came into their thirties amid a worldwide eco-nomic depression that is omitted from this story of prosperity, of moving away from poverty. Early-twen-tieth-century Chile saw no shortage of dissent and unrest, based in part on the demands of workers, including recent immigrants from Europe, to have a greater share in the nation's wealth. *Always from Somewhere Else* portrays a number of those immigrants, skilled artisans engaged in trade and thus excluded from the aristocratic elite. In *Cuando era Muchacho,* spirited memoirs of the years leading up to 1920, about the same time Abraham's older brother Marcos arrived in Valparaíso, Chilean writer José Santos González Vera, also the son of a European immigrant, describes how the children of merchants were excluded from secon-dary schools because money earned in business was considered tainted, whereas money in the form of promissory notes bearing honorable family names was not. He describes, too, the heated discussions of various anarchist philosophies among the shoemakers and other guild workers. González Vera's own enterprise combined these modes. As a vendor of books and subscriptions, he would spy potential clients in the post office, follow and harangue them from the door down to the steps to the sidewalk and even onto the streetcar, until they bought his wares. It is instructive to consider that the atheist González Vera, son of a Spanish father, with Catholic parents, became a writer and urban organizer while his contemporary, Abraham Agosín the tailor, a permanent foreigner and a Jew, steered clear of politics and religion and became a bastion of middle-class Quillota.

The sign of the tailor's relative independence and class aspirations is his watch, which Abraham acquired in 1910, marking his status as a professional not bound to the industrial time clock or to the rhythms of communal labor. A watch-owner has time to keep track of, to wind up and set; and is his or her own boss. Also fundamental to the tailor's trade, above and beyond skills in math and design and the possession of a degree of capital with which to purchase cloth and supplies, is the practice of courtesy and the ability to listen, for the tailor works with the public. For the sake of business in a provincial town, the tailor will be one of the more cosmopolitan members, coming into regular contact with traveling salespeople—Turks, Lebanese—selling cloth and sundries. More aware of the world than most, in Quillota a tailor would be an arbiter of fashion, although not for the "good families" that brought their clothes in Santiago. Charged with measuring, cutting, and stitching the better run of cloth, a tailor must be absolutely trustworthy as far as delivery is concerned. The tailor is among the more mobile of businesspersons, coming into daily contact with people from across the range of social classes; his or her wealth is based in that contact, and in the stock of cloth, rather than in land or heavy machinery. With a prosperity based in ongoing relationships and in trust, a tailor must be discreet: Abraham the Jewish tailor of Quillota therefore knows not just to listen, *"con cautela,"* but also to teach his sons likewise to absorb, through silent watchful attention, the circumference of speech. His youngest son Moisés, especially, practices and perfects this art of listening, attending lectures without taking notes, teaching in turn his daughter, who brings to the living the messages of the dead.

While Abraham, engaged in a quarrel with God, belongs to no synagogue, he is nonetheless known as the charitable Jewish tailor of Quillota. His older brother Marcos hides his Jewishness and embraces the Masonic brotherhood, which was one of the most effectively organized of Chile's secular groups, its members known politically as radicals because they were so committed to the separation of church and state. Their efforts contributed to the election of reformists such as Presidents Alessandri (in 1925) and Pedro Aguirre Cerda (in 1938). The Masons were an antifascist "international brotherhood," which is why they came under attack—along with Jews, and along with Jehovah's Witnesses (as conscientious objectors), gypsies (Sinta), and open homosexuals—when National Socialism came to power in Germany in 1933. In Chile supporters of the right wing looked to the overtly pro-German army to counter the power of Masons and the radicals: while the army declared itself nationalistic and "apolitical," its leader, Carlos Ibañez, minister of defense, sought political power throughout the twenties, gaining the presidency first in 1929, and then again in 1954. The combination of blatant authoritarianism and deepening economic crisis brought down the Ibañez regime in 1932, but Chile's return to constitutional government in the following year did not lessen the threat of a right-wing, pro-German, anti-Semitic military takeover. Even as Moisés Agosín prepared to enter high school, civil sectors directed by professionals formed the Republican Militia, which was armed and practiced maneuvers. Although Colonel Ibañez's coup attempt in 1934 did not succeed, fascism was openly acceptable in September of 1938. As Moisés Agosín studied to enter the University of Chile, where he would be one of three Jews among a thousand medical students, a group of young National Socialists gathered first in the University of Chile to organize a Nazi-style putsch in front of the Moneda, the president's residence in Santiago: sixty-three young students were killed (Villalobos 353).

Argentina and Chile had been virtually untouched by World War I. This would not be the case in World

War II. Officially "neutral," the nations of the "Southern Cone" of Latin America (Argentina, Brazil, Uruguay, Chile) were divided between long-term economic ties to Axis countries and intense diplomatic pressure exerted by an increasingly powerful United States. Where Argentina in the 1920s was moving towards the exaggerated nationalism that culminated in military rule from 1930 to 1943, Chile was relatively open, as evidenced by the rise of "radicalism," the new, democratic constitution of 1925, and the wider inclusion of the new middle class in the country's political life. Within that middle class, the Jewish communities in Argentina have always been much larger and more influential, in real numbers and in percentages of the general population, than in Chile. Geography is a principal factor: how much more intrepid to sail from Europe to Chile, instead of stopping in Buenos Aires. The cliché of Chile as a paradise appears in one traveler's description when the American Jewish Congress saw the need, in 1939, to provide information about countries not just of refuge, but possibly of long-term settlement, in the event of an Axis victory (Cohen). Contradicting this notion of the Chilean paradise were the experiences of refugee doctors arriving in Santiago: as *Always from Somewhere Else* recounts, these specialists trained in Vienna and Hamburg were not allowed to practice in the city, but were sent off to the provinces.

## II. Mosaic Displacements, or the Search
## for Knowledge

### Quillota

Where Valparaíso is turned towards the sea, Quillota and other inland towns are more typical of Chile's population centers. Originally fortified settlements in the valleys, these towns boast at least one church for every neighborhood, the largest one fronting a plaza that on an early Sunday evening will fill up with teenagers strolling the side streets, in groups of four and five, divided by sex, while the older folk sit in pairs on the benches, watching over it all, and groups of men in their twenties cluster around the entrances to the small general stores that sell everything from cigarettes and milk to hats and canes. The lottery ticket sellers call out; courting couples eat ice-cream; and parents or older siblings stand in line with young children to buy balloons. It is in the plaza that the relative prosperity and values of a small city like Quillota are revealed: respect for commercial success is overridden by the profound desire to seem no different from one's neighbors, who are all watching from benches, from the bandstand in the plaza, and through the slats of the drawn blinds of their houses.

Taking a bus straight through towns and cities such as Quillota offers nothing by way of conventional tourism, but it will reveal the economic and social interests of the entire surrounding countryside. For all appearances, the visitor could be in any provincial, traditional city of the Spanish-speaking world: Saragoza, in Spain; Uruapán, in Mexico. The bus will seem to stay forever, for the driver will want to greet friends, showing all the world that he is employed and is no man's slave. He will linger to enjoy at least two cigarettes, a hamburger, and some snack from a wrapper, asserting his citizen's right to sunset socializing–a right and a pleasure that Raquel, Abraham, and their older children had to earn, for it was not automatically granted them.

The narrative's attention to Quillota over the course of fifty years, from the 1930s to 1980s, imparts a clear sense of who the "personages" would be in such a provincial city: the mayor, the school principal, the police chief, the high school janitor. We learn, too, of the groups who have substantial, behind-the-scenes influence: the German club, the Salesian fathers, whose power is all the more accentuated by the fact that this is the center of an agricultural region where ownership of the land does not change. The presence of so many churches, and especially a cathedral, suggests a contingent of large landowners who have made Quillota a stronghold, a base of operations. Agosín captures quite well the arrogance of the bigwigs and club members toward the rest of the citizens, who "were branded as communists, impostors, and poorly dressed and shabby eccentrics," indicating the political parameters of class and taste and conformity.

Quillota in the 1930s would have been well-to-do. By way of its isolation and the concentration of land ownership, the Quillota of Moisés Agosín's adolescence would have been immune to the organized strikes of the cities and mining areas. The influence of the Catholic Church and the existence of prestigious clubs from which the Agosíns were excluded tells us that these *latifundos* (big farms) in Chile's agricultural heartland would be among the last to be divided. Merchants such as the Agosíns would be more accepted by second-generation members of the middle class, who held secure, if poorly paid, civil service jobs: secondary school teachers, porters, groundskeepers, municipal guards. Not in companionship with other children but in the comprehension and solidarity of such public employees would Moisés Agosín encounter a haven from persecution, finding the best math teachers and poets, for the profession of public school teacher in Chile was still at that time a respectable, although underpaid one, offering a steady salary and a kind of protection for intellectuals and artists. This narrative is full of gratitude, as is right, for the integrity and kindness of those teachers whose profound competence and fairness counters the perfidy of false, hypocritical teachers, the taskmasters who are militarists in disguise, enforcers of conformity and guardians of mediocrity. The sinister side of "peaceable Quillota" appears in the dualism of the two sons of the most popular man in town, the school janitor. One is the shadowy, forlorn Willi, whose brother was a torturer, an assassin who accused Willi when confronted with the facts of his crimes. While his father had a funeral attended by hundreds of former students, Willi is sad, lost, a forgotten man. Just as there is no place for Willi in the new Chile, he would be similarly exiled, isolated, friendless in the old one.

Through the medium of music Raquel and her youngest son, Moisés, break through the barriers that the conservative forces of Quillota erect against them. Singing Raquel gives voice to what she virtually forbids within her house. The world, the languages that she has put behind, reappear in her French, Turkish, Russian verses ringing through the civic festivities. Moisés slips into the darkness of the silent movie theater to sit at the piano. Its strings and hammers stun the assembled, scarcely comprehending crowd with the agony of his isolation and the certainty of his dreams.

## Santiago

Combining music with science and mathematics, Moisés Agosín seeks out an education of the spirit, rejecting superstition and replicating the best of nineteenth-century liberalism: the enlightenment legacy of science, work, empirical truth, mistrust of ecclesiastical authority, benign atheism. Combined with the caution and discretion learned from Abraham, this education will be Moisés's shield when he moves from Quillota to the University of Chile in 1940, finding himself quite literally in a medieval dungeon whose guardians are would-be alchemists and magicians and a landlady with a mysterious ailment that leads her to attend mass throughout the week and suffer in the night for the sin of giving lodging to a well-paying Jewish medical student. His best friend is "Luchito," the skeleton purchased from a local gravedigger, his comrade in anatomy lessons.

Replacing the romance of origins is a kind of subtle comedy as the search for knowledge increasingly centers around Dr. Agosín's fascination with flies and parasites, even as the doctors around him, "alchemists" obsessed with encountering the philosopher's stone, present an approach to pharmacy that stresses the memorization of medicinal substances. The positivist philosophy of these alchemists presumes finite, unchanging knowledge as opposed to the experimental method, which assumes that one learns through inquiry, trial and error, the testing of hypotheses. The Chilean (ultimately, Spanish) system's philosophical premise is that medicine could be a profession if the doctor's training resembled, without challenging, the work of the priest, the doctor of souls. These and other precepts—including the notion that good doctors will possess the proper bloodlines and pieties—are totally alien to the world of the laboratory, yet the secret fraternity of doctors from "old families," the Academy of San Lucas, prevails during World War II, when superbly qualified refugee doctors driven from Europe are likewise driven from Santiago. Such anti-Semitism in the medical profession is not limited to Chile: in the United States, the

Albert Einstein College of Medicine was established in the 1950s in response to quotas and blatantly exclusionary practices directed against Jews.

In Santiago the voices of father and daughter come together. The tone is sad, more angry than bitter, irrevocably cognizant of the network of powerful social forces that regards secular teaching, science, and medicine as potential threats to the power of tradition. In civic construction, what belongs to the nation's primary identity, the Catholic churches, are given the utmost priority, while the design, maintenance, and repair of the teaching hospital is stalled and trashed. On a practical level, the people who run the country will go abroad for advanced schooling and treatment. The narrative in Santiago furthermore instances the peculiarly sinister shape that "conscience" takes. The fondness for bonhomie brings "friends" to Dr. Agosín's house, to share his family's table and drink his wine, but not to make a public stand on his behalf, their hypocrisy revealed when the "ethical" consideration of his Jewishness leads them to withhold support for his candidacy for a full professorship. Giving the nod to his idea of founding an association of research doctors, they form the association in his absence, thus excluding him, and no other university doctor, from the roster. In the early 1960s, during the Six-Day War between Israel and Egypt, the "friends" profess to share concern for "his country," which he at that point had yet even to visit. In the later sixties, it is the friendly, well-meaning colleagues of Dr. Agosín who give him the greatest impetus to leave, suggesting that until he joins the left wing he will be perhaps rightly suspect as an imperialist, for his research is funded by U.S.–based foundations. Following the overt politicization of hospitals under Allende (1970–1973) is the fascist takeover of medicine and, under Pinochet, beginning in 1973, the horrifying complicity of doctors assisting in torture sessions. Seeking freedom by working abroad, Dr. Moisés Agosín will find that the discoveries of an experimental scientist from the Third World are regarded as legitimate only when Euro-American investigators can appropriate them as their own.

The passion for science is poetry, the sense that hidden systems of knowledge will come to light through minute observation. Commitment to close, dispassionate study, rigorous examination, and adherence to human ethics help explain this narrative's lack of rancor. A mosaic is created through fractures, displacements, and picking up the pieces in the search for knowledge. A variety of times and locales are arranged and put to the microscope. The doctor-biochemist-pianist's principled search for palpable knowledge stands as the sole alternative to the twisted paths of pseudo-scientisms and xenophobic, racist ideologies encountered in central Chile from 1930 to the present, in Washington D.C. embassy parties in the 1950s, in Georgia in the 1970s.

## WHERE IS GOD'S HOUSE?

*Divisions in Jewish Communities*

Walking the streets of Santiago, Moisés Agosín points to the effects of borders even within the tiny Jewish community in Chile, with its separate synagogues depending on nations. Such a division was by no means limited to Chile: in 1941, the thousand Jews of Lima, Peru, had three different synagogues (Cohen). In 1942, the tiny Jewish settlement of Sosua, in the Dominican Republic, with less than five hundred people, formed into factions such as the Luxembourgers, the Belgians, and the French (Papernik). Rejecting nationalisms (which inevitably lead to war) and class hatred (which overlooks that capacity for cruelty that rich and poor possess in like measure), we can begin to understand and share in the victorious survival of Moisés Agosín, a "Third World" scientist who triumphs over medievalism, a child of the Enlightenment. Although he is a secular Jew who tells his six-year-old daughter as she emerges, naked as Eve, from her bath, that "God was invented by others," Moisés Agosín is nonetheless a believer: he believes in the avatars of music, which include scrupulous science, healing medicine, the orchestra of the laboratory, the devotion of family and friends. This power of belief, this faith, counters the racial theories of the Nazis, which were above all else impersonal. Fascinated with measurement, they sought a fixity of categories of types that no conversation, reciprocity, or exchange could penetrate.

The narrator reminds us that there is a persistent

identification with Germany among Chilean descendants of German-speaking settlers, whether originating with the emigrants that the government of President Manuel Montt actively courted from 1834 onwards, or with the shipload of refugees barred entry to Argentina, subsequently landing in Valparaíso in 1939 (Cohen). Chileans from families who identify with their German background continue to think of themselves as German, whether fifty or one hundred and fifty years have passed since the earliest arrivals. What *Always from Somewhere Else* notes of present-day Chile holds true for much of Latin America, where German alliances remain in the form of tourism, investment, political ties and intracommunal marriages. The visibility and acceptance of these ties contrast strongly with the atmosphere of scant toleration and frequent rejection of Jews in similar roles: in political and economic summits, the Germans are given the front seats, and the Jews, the row at the back.

At work in "German-Chilean" identity is not only the phenomenon of intracommunal marriage—the tendency for newer settlers from Germany to marry the descendants of settlers from an earlier era—but also a willful forgetting of the past, as is clear in "Sea Voyages," one of this book's many embedded narratives. Taking a stance seen elsewhere in her work, Marjorie Agosín becomes the almost-invisible observer of Germans outside of Germany, showing how the torturers and the tortured are forever drawn together by a history of roles repeated and re-enacted, generation after generation. The section on Auschwitz lists the questions that each generation must ask: why did I survive, where do I come from, where is God's true house? In the length and breadth of Agosín's work we are constantly reminded that the land of Chile is spread with cemeteries, in a string of gravesites variously recognized or ignored. The names of these cemeteries—Belloto, Conchalí, Pisagua—are inscribed less in a tradition of graveside memorial or mourning than in an attempt to grasp the relation of a vanishing past to a profoundly mortal present in which violent, unforeseen change is not only possible, but likely.

### III. OF SPEECH, SILENCE, AND THE EXILE OF MEMORY

#### SPEECH AND LISTENING

The book of meditation and memory is not linear, not direct, but fragmentary, looping back and repeating the already said, discovering the omitted in the known, constantly remaking the map of the past. In the course of learning to listen to silence the book crosses from dictation, a setting down of the testimonies of others, into a meditation on how the rush into modernity is rendered barbarous if there is no attention to justice. Amid the act of meditative listening and subsequently recording what that living voice reveals, the hand turns the page, crossing oceans, flying across the night. The hand moves toward and across the map of the world, seeking out a place of meeting, a place to enact a ceremony of witness in which the Holocaust is not unique, for the use of torture and techniques of mass intimidation do not end with 1945.

This book is for the present and for the future, for what Majorie Agosín has called "the encounter between the lives and deaths of the survivors of the European or Latin American Holocaust." Listening to the stories of the persecution of Jews in Europe, listening to the dissidents and others who suffered under Pinochet, reveals the ad-men's lie of "we all advance together in order and peace." In the journey towards reconciliation, in this narrative's necessary return to honor the dead and the living, we meet impoverished, dignified teachers, brilliant scientists, craven administrators, janitors, businessmen, Masons, singers, traveling to ports, to cemeteries, provincial houses, expanding cities, and urbane parties, and dwelling, too, in the humiliations of exile.

Where Agosín's earlier book of family memoirs, *A Cross and a Star,* works to present from within the childhood of a Jewish girl, the writer's mother, amid the German-Chilean landlords and the dispossessed Mapuche of the south of Chile, the present book is a more complex, more consciously crafted account. One beginning is the romance of origins, moving from the writer's paternal grandparents in the Crimea to the last of their new beginnings, the house in Quillota where they raised their youngest son, the writer's father.

Another beginning is Moisés Agosín's transition from adolescence into adulthood, for the writer focuses on identity's evolution, factoring in family history and habits and customs within broader historical events such as the Holocaust and the politics of the Cold War. Where the earlier volume of memoirs is a family history that stretches to include the memories of the various Indian and mixed-blood women who worked in her parents' and grandparents' houses, this latter book is the story of how the youngest son of immigrant Jews, a tailor and a singer and cigarette-maker, persevered despite the blatantly anti-Semitic medical and educational establishments of Chile and went on to become an internationally recognized research scientist. Where the earlier book details the popularity of Nazism among the German enclaves of Southern Chile and the day-to-day exclusions that made up the experience of the children in the four Jewish families of Osorno, Chile, the present book describes a far lonelier childhood, in which the boy's only friendships were with a few public school teachers brave enough to encourage the youngest son of the town's only Jews.

## SILENCE AND SPEECH

*Always from Somewhere Else* continues Marjorie Agosín's longstanding production of books composed in collaboration with others. Like a range of Latin American women, the best-known example being Mexican writer

Elena Poniatowska, Agosín has a long history of working with testimonial literature, a mode which has done much to focus attention on the lives of Latin American women not previously associated with print culture.

Not enough has been written about how the necessarily collaborative enterprise of producing books—especially those that work with translation and testimony, with the juncture of writing with speech—is bound up with problems of class privilege and unequal access to print. Translation and testimony are forms that can actually reinforce the very notions of authority that such work purports seeking to change. When a privileged speaker appropriates another person's other-wise silent voice to her own, instead of "giving voice" to those who suffer, the writer-editor actually confirms the muteness of the person being "spoken for."

In the present text, however, the writer never represents herself as "speaking for" another. She instead points out that she has had to intuit much of the stories here told, because Moisés Agosín, like his father Abraham, is a man of few words. While that habit of cautionary silence, born of necessity, might have contributed to the subject's survival and success, it creates gaps in knowledge, which distance the writer from her subject, as in the enigma of the name *Agosín,* borrowed or invented en route from Odessa to Istanbul. That search for knowledge is also Moisés Agosín's search, as his final encounter with his mother reveals in the riddle of her deathbed answer when he asks her about the origins of their name.

Because the writer, in telling such stories, distinguishes where the father's and daughter's experiences are separate and where conjoined, what emerges here is less an artificially constructed unified single voice than a litany of the dead and the living. Such recounting of past and present is, as the book's prologue poses, an acknowledgment of the need to move beyond lamentation.

## COMPOSING THE EXILE

Refusing to live in the judgments of others, refusing to engage in exclusivism, embracing cosmopolitanism, eschewing borders or cultural identities derived from the perceptions of others, the narrative records and borrows the exiles of the Agosíns. That loan is assimilated to the sufferings of other ordinary, too readily forgotten Chileans: not just the disappeared, during the years of the Pinochet dictatorship, but the one million Chileans, one in fourteen, who took up residence abroad in the years 1973 to 1989. The linking of these exiles and displacements forges a human chain, from the prodigious wanderers Abraham and Raquel to their youngest child and now to their grandchildren and great-grandchildren, who inhabit and leave behind a series of provisional yet well-loved houses and apartments. That a residence is temporary does not diminish the joys experienced therein.

With the resources of the tailor, who knows how to listen, to observe, to cut and stitch cloth, and the audacity of the singer, whose macaronic verses bear the evidence of her exiles, we too are carried from port to port. In the production of the arpeggio, the hand's strength and precision finds the equivalent to the singer's vibrato. As a pianist, Moisés produces "melodies that seem to fly away from his hands like a breeze, like a piece of velvet on feast days." Moisés and those who listen to him "with care" would know both the tension of the arpeggio and the relief of it being finished.

Some items have been deliberately disguised, or put in a different order, to give narrative sense to an abundantly lived existence. Like the grandmother Raquel, the narrator-daughter is here a scribe: as in Isabel Allende's novel, *La Casa de los Espiritus,* as in Lorna Dee Cervantes's book of poems, *Emplumada,* as in Anzia Yezierska's novel *The Bread Givers,* the daughter/granddaughter negotiates the world. In *Always from Somewhere Else,* however, the point is less to order or bring messages from the past, or to serve as a medium between the older generation and the surrounding, foreign world, or to locate oneself in the New World, than it is to put oneself in order. While some might argue that language is what makes us fully human, in these pages language is but a subsidiary—at first a handmaiden, then betrothed, in the latter chapters—to memory. The marriage of language and memory is an arrow shot into the future as a century of persecution, flights, and (for some) movement toward new lands draws towards a close. The introspection of the relatively sedentary granddaughter is very rare in Chilean literature, where history and autobiography have always been overwhelmingly oriented toward the outside. Even the great, introspective poet Neruda devotes more space, in his memoirs, to colorful inventories of friendships, meals, and proudly amassed wealth than to the past as a place, a home for memory, a catalog of desires. With Chile having become, in the 1990s, so intently, aggressively prosperous, a neo-Liberal model for all Latin America, it is important to remember the impermanence of that prosperity. The record here translated from Spanish and published in the United States is a valuable reminder of an always shifting world in which memory has a place, its own place—defining, separating the living from the dead, yet joining us with those no longer alive.

Unlike the family memoir, a genre often bedecked by piety, motivated by sentiment, and mired in the attempt to justify present power, this book re-enacts the past as part of an ongoing and universal search for justice. That search requires travel: local power has no interest in addressing past wrongs. In place of real justice, local and would-be national powers would urge us into false travels, cynically presenting the deportations of Haitians, of Mexicans, of Hungarian gypsies, Quiche Maya Indians, European Jews, as necessary steps along a "new road," in fact, identical to the old one in its trail of hunger, exploitation, long hours, low pay, extermination. As the past recedes, the sooner to forget the persistence of injustice, the twentieth century gallops to a close. In the absence of denunciation, every sign indicates that this peace is a sham and showy merchandise distributed to a few. Economic injustice is the cost of an absolute amnesia: the ten surnames who three, five generations ago ruled Chile still rule today.

## MEMORY AND IDENTITY: THE HISTORIAN'S CHOICE

The craft of social history was in the 1930s a shining part of Chile's extraordinary rich intellectual scene, yet even as writers such as Domingo Amunátegui Solar argued that "the anonymous individual whose work, muted and ongoing . . . contributes more than the illustrious personages to the greatness and decadence of a people," he and his followers dismissed the non-Europeans, mestizos especially, as "fit only for farm labor" (Amunátegui 7). This book's meditation on memory and identity concentrates on the period from 1930 to the present, alternating between the political turmoil of the 1940s and the 1960s, the stability of the 1950s, and finally the privations and terrors of Chile's seventeen-year dictatorship. It is a history that many writers in contemporary Chile would prefer to leave behind. No other book of memoirs has spanned, and few books of history even now acknowledge, the continuity between the repression of minorities in democratic Chile and the repression of the dictatorship.

While Chile's bastions of male historians would do

well to return to Amunátegui after having been mired
for two decades in a feverish attempt to prove, via the
eighteenth and nineteenth centuries, that the nation equals
the state, the best historians of moment are journalists
such as Patricia Policer, anthropologists such as Sonia
Montecinos, and poets such as Marjorie Agosín. The
faithful documentation of individual stories and experiences works to reconstruct the texture of daily life, and
to illuminate the values (or lack of them) by which people live. By producing books that detail and move
past the bitter and divided history of Latin America, it
becomes possible to contribute to the project of explor-
ing identity's relation to the irony of history.

While filled with love and longing for the "paradise"
that well-to-do Chileans and foreigners have experienced
in Chile, the author's awareness of herself and her
family as survivors keeps this from being a nostalgic book.
In the attempt to seek justice, we experience the texture of life in this physically beautiful, utterly divided,
polite and hospitable land. We see the dual face of Chile:
the face that is wide-open, turned toward foreigners, a
nation of "European" traditions and frank emulation of
the newest modes from abroad, and then the blind side,
as revealed in the life-narrative of Moisés Agosín,
medical student and internationally recognized scientist. Chile's obsessive concerns with "good origins," "good
name" (one that is known and familiar), "good family"
(patriarchal), with appearances and with "what people
will say," means that Moisés Agosín enrolls his daugh-

ters in a Hebrew secondary school and tells them that
God was invented by other people.

The history of immigrants, whatever their destina-
tions, reveals that countries are invented, not made, and
that they are rarely shared. As the grandchild of
refugees who escaped the madness of Hitler, Marjorie
Agosín writes firmly within and against the rich, complex cultural histories of twentieth-century Chilean
and U.S. immigrant literature and biography. As the Latin
American daughter of European Jews settled in Chile,
subsequently emigrating to the United States, she
offers us a balanced critique of a century of displacements and borrowed exiles. Her second volume of
family memoirs is in the best tradition of oral history,
combining memory and written testimony. Governed
by the critical intelligence, the observing eyes, the
voices of three generations of survivors, this history of
displaced persons knowingly invents countries. Through
a combination of stories recounted with names and dates,
with personal testimony, it counters the very reduced
history of Chile, whose object is to maintain the priv-
ileges of a class that feels itself the natural rulers of those
with darker skins, state school educations, poor health,
and scant property. Where positivist history contents
itself with detailing the roots of Chile's road to socialism
and its bloody right-wing coup, the intertwined testimonies of Moisés and Marjorie Agosín tell a different
story, in which the oligarchs who controlled and still
control Chile have little or nothing to do with the

day-to-day lives of their fellow citizens, who do not sit at tables attended by servants, who have never traveled on airplanes.

## IV. IDENTITY'S IRONIES, OR A COMEDY OF LISTS

The commitment to documentation, investigation, and to comedy makes *Always from Somewhere Else* the strongest, surest, and most ambitious of Agosín's volumes to date. It looks closely at the difficult problem of New World–Old World identity, in relation to religion, language, nationalism, migration. The narrative argues strongly for the importance of place in memory. The writer takes care not to identify her voice with her father's, and to separate the strands of what she has experienced, directly, in childhood, from what she has learned from the stories of others and made her own through retelling. All of these distinctions are vital to the task of making sense of that modern and irrational notion of "national identity."

### THE IRONY OF BELONGING TO A MINORITY WITHIN A MINORITY

Moisés Agosín and his family have enjoyed relative economic security in equal measure with social exclusion. The discrimination directed against them does not vanish with a change in residence from Chile to the United States; only the moorings shift. In Chile, family connections and "name" are everything, so they are excluded as Jews. Among U.S. and Western European researchers, Moisés Agosín is dismissed as a "Third World" scientist. His children, living in the United States South, are taunted for being "Latinos."

## THE IRONIES OF SIMILARITY IN DIFFERENCE

How does a daughter less dedicated to the waltzes of Lizst or Chopin than to the "avocado and toast" sold in the music conservatory cafeteria, a daughter who declares herself incapable of addition or subtraction, understand a father whose twin passions are classical piano and the microscopic study of bugs and parasites? The meeting of the two occurs in the poet's combining of humor and understatement with *"los gestos de amor"*—the gestures or acts of love (a term Agosín employs in her poetry). In her quest to understand identity, the scientist's daughter deciphers the elaborate codes of intimacy, pointing to disloyalties and celebrating the values of loyalty, disinterested charity, and nonconformity, revisiting her own and her father's and her grandparents' adolescent years—in the friendlessness of Georgia, in noisy summer parties in the beach towns of Quisco, in the silence of provincial Quillota, in the raw newness of Odessa, and in the cemeteries where she converses with her dead.

## THE IRONIES OF "MY COUNTRY"

Moisés Agosín's story studies the particular twists of anti-Semitism in Chile (likewise evident in Argentina), which rests upon unspoken pacts between a conservative Catholic hierarchy, wealthy landowners, and German industrialists. The writer uses over and over again the phrase *my country*. For her, there is no doubt that the referent is Chile, but for Moisés Agosín that referent is less clear. When Dr. Agosín is mugged on a visit to Santiago, the thieves return his Visa gold card, embarrassed that they have attacked a foreigner. The question of what Moisés Agosín's country is constitutes one of the principal preoccupations of this book. His childhood and his daughter's resound with an anti-Semitism so deeply embedded in the culture that it emerges in children's songs ("Who stole the bread from the oven? The Jewish dogs, the Jewish dogs"). The isolation of his adolescence forces him to study, to turn to the two outlets of music and medicine. Yet the harder he works to move beyond the life of a merchant, the more of a threat he apparently poses—thus the scorn, the knife he is forced to carry, the anonymous phone threats in the night. A paradox of identity is that Moisés Agosín's Jewishness is defined less by his membership in a Jewish community, than by the exclusionary nationalism that asserts that he is somehow not Chilean. The problem is an ongoing one: even after democracy has returned to Chile, there yet remains the elusive sense that some people will always be foreign. This was articulated by a Chilean student of mine, whose surname was Slavic and first name was French, who had lived two decades abroad, and who said to me: "Agosín? She is a foreigner. Because of her name."

The ultimate irony of identity is that the condition of being an outsider strips bare hypocrisy as well as "true" devotion and piety. Other memoirs of "outsiders" in Chile—German immigrant Eva Krauthein's account of her twenty-odd years, from 1945 to 1965, comes to mind, as does U.S. Ambassador Claude Bower's *Behind Embassy Doors*—do not work with this insight, in part because these writers prefer not to take on the head- and hair-splitting question of nationalism's role in identity formation. The life and experience of Moisés Agosín, however distinct from his parents' lives, is nonetheless the experience of an outsider, someone repeatedly excluded.

By centering on immigrant experience, on exile, on reclusions, on the obscured lives of women such as Grandmother Raquel who fills her notebooks with Spanish-Cyrillic jottings, Agosín points to the limitations that "good society" imposes. One of her central topics is the hypocrisy of discrimination and racism, whether manifest in prejudice against Jews in Chile, the official denial of Chilean *mestizaje* by dark-skinned military attachés, the use of non-whites for cruel medical experimentation in Latin America and in the U.S. South, or the obstacles that scientists from Latin America experience in trying to get their work recognized in Europe and North America. These bland denials and mindless cruelties reveal the narrowness and inhumanity of the mindset necessary to producing a single, homogenous, national identity.

## THE IRONY OF NOSTALGIA

It is hard to avoid nostalgia for Chile, for its landscapes absolutely without equivalent in the world, for the luminescence of a sky in which the sun every day struggles past the wall of the Andes and later falls into an ocean with no land in sight (a luminescence that in Santiago is permanently clouded by exhaust). To be a refugee in Chile requires real determination, and not just because the winds buffeting the coast are the least predictable in the world. Descending from a boat docked in Valparaíso, the refugee encounters dust, desert, mud, a land facing the ocean and backed by the wall of the Andes. The refugee from Europe shares with the emigrant from the countryside the head-on rejection of those who are already established in the cities, where every barrio overflows with aspirants to the status of *"gente bien,"* focused on consumption. Not qualifications but family connections and friendships ensure the physician's success.

Faced with the dilemma of how to charge patients whose illness is caused by poverty, Moisés Agosín opts instead for a career in research, receiving money from international foundations, from the United States, and eventually moving there, so that *Always from Somewhere Else* is written within U.S. territory, within "a country of polls"—that is, of classifications, of stereotypes created here, as in Chile, to justify continued feudalism. Where the feudalism of Chile is expressed by the arrogance of the oligarchy and the influence of the Church, the feudalism of the United States, expressed by proprietors and local landowners, produces neighborhoods of closed houses at dusk. If we are to understand how humanity can survive the mediocre consumerism that threatens to be the defining aspect of U.S. culture, we could do worse than to turn to this fortunate narrative, which offers a wealth of alternatives.

Elizabeth Rosa Horan
Tempe, Arizona
June 1998

## WORKS CITED

Amunátegui Solar, Domingo. *Historia social de Chile.* Santiago: Nascimento, 1932.

Bowers, Claude Gernade. *Chile Through Embassy Windows 1939–1953.* New York: Simon and Schuster, 1958.

Cohen, Jacob Xenab. *Jewish Life in South America: A Survey Study for the American Jewish Congress.* Foreword by Stephen S. Wise. New York: Bloch Publishing Co., 1941.

Góngora, Mario. *Ensayo histórico sobre la noción de estado en Chile en los siglos xix yxx.* Santiago: Editorial Universitaria, 1992.

González Vera, José Santos. *Cuando era Muchacho.* Santiago: Nascimento, 1951.

Krauthein, Eva. *Paradise Found and Lost: Odyssey in Chile.* Albuquerque, New Mexico: Amador Publishers, 1994.

Papernik, Otto. Unpublished manuscript. Sosua, Dominican Republic: n.d. (1970s).

Villalobos, Sergio. *Chile y su historia.* Santiago: Editorial Universitaria, 1993.

Wojak, Irmtrud. *Exil in Chile. Die Deutsch-Jüdische und Politsche Emigration wahrend des Nationalsozialismus 1933–1945.* Berlin: Metropol Verlag, 1994.

# PROLOGUE

*Crossings*

My father was born in Marseilles
because they expelled
his brothers from Istanbul
and his parents
from Odessa.

He came to Chile by boat
and lived in Quillota,
destroyed by
three earthquakes,
then in Santiago,
where they threw him out of the boarding houses
and student dormitories.

He emigrated to the
United States,
where no one turned him away,
but everyone saw him
walking the earth
as a stranger.

*Crossings*

I write these buried and half-recovered memories of my
father and I sit close to him, examining his eyes and his
fragile body, never meant for war. His calm voice is like
that of the birds who sojourn in cloudy regions as I feel
his presence amidst the silence of the shadows. Then
I know that he has returned home. The words that we
randomly utter are both sad and sweet, replete with fall-
en angels and lost navigators.

In my father's eyes I can see all of the voyages: Odessa,
Istanbul, Marseilles, Valparaíso, Quillota, Santiago,
the United States of America. His gaze conjures up images
of struggle, shattered zones of pain. I approach his tenderness and hear the cries of my grandparents walking
barefoot toward the false vessels of peace.

I look at my father and sense that I am also a mixture of these voyages. I am like lost nights at sea, like
a ship without sails or figurehead. My ancestors have
bestowed upon me the accumulated grief of persecution and exile and the strident happiness that arises from
being alive and able to say "thank you" and *"l'chaim"*
in the mornings. So I write what cannot be said, and the

buried words spring forth out of the subtle silence of one who has learned to listen.

As I write my father's memoirs, as I reinvent the past and the unsteady future, I am forever thankful that my father did not succumb inside the barbed-wire of the camps. Before he was born, my father's parents had journeyed from Odessa to Istanbul and then to Marseilles, France. My father was born in 1922 in a rundown hospital in Marseilles, in a dark public ward. When he was three years old—before the Nazis stormed through Europe—the good star of fortune carried him across the seas to Valparaíso, Chile, barefoot and numb from the cold, and then to the small town of Quillota, where he grew up on fertile soil, amid grapes and avocados and too many churches. He travelled to the capital of Santiago to study medicine, to be, once again, the only Jew in his class. Finally, the terrors of the Chilean military dictatorship drove him to his final place of exile, the United States, where he was suddenly not only a Jew but also a "Hispanic."

Today I narrate his great book of life. Retelling his story at last, after hearing it so many times, I take up my role in a fragmented memory play that will also become part of my son Joseph's heritage.

I listen to my father and my thoughts unite with his. Together we dismantle absences and form arches with the words of silence, the voice that returns like memory and beseeches like a bird or a vast golden prayer.

I write this book of memories without any answers,

for I, too, am a survivor. I am the daughter of Moisés Agosín of Marseilles and the granddaughter of Abraham Agosín of Sebastopol.

# ORIGINS

From Sebastopol to Valparaiso

1910–1926

## The Wanderers

And they were always from somewhere else, abandoning the burning villages, grasping to the sacred rituals of memory. My grandparents wrapped up the braids of garlic, preserving their ancient beliefs and the rhythm of their meals. The village of flying fish and Chagalian portraits disappeared like a tottering deck of cards because this is how it is written in the great book of life.

We are a wandering people, treasuring the days of all our returns, searching for recovered lands brimming with promises as we arrive everywhere and nowhere. Always filled with the frontiers that exist between the familiar and the distant, we remember inversely certain itineraries of homes that have been burned to the ground, books about God and our own plundered memories. But we always search for a new horizon, where we may stop to build a dream, a beginning that lies beyond all the shadows.

A roaming people, a people of abandoned doors and beatings in the middle of the night, our history is submerged in the mysterious book of God. We are and are not those who flee at all times, making a ladder of stars with clean hands that have not killed but have only been tied. Hence, we arrive everywhere and invent utopias and new languages as we continue the trek, moved by our own history, always ready to leave at the appointed hour with the belongings of memory and time.

## My Grandparents

We never were able to find out in which forest or garden they had met and first gazed at each other. They did remember that it was the time of the almond blossoms, when the rivers were filled with fragrances that surrounded lonely adolescents who were accustomed to inventing love.

This is how my grandparents spoke of Odessa, a misty and radiant, refined and sinister city in the Ukraine. Their names were Abraham and Raquel. They were young and in love in the year 1910.

My grandparents met in some restless and secluded place, in that city of forests and water by the sea. Abraham and Raquel, two timid workers toiling in solitude, two Jews passing through a city that was foreign to them, confused by the wind with its shadowy secrets. Odessa, so clean and agitated after the rain and the pogroms, so strange after the wars.

Since their childhoods, Abraham and Raquel were tattooed by the destiny of their impoverished ancestry and of the forsaken, even though the spirit and breath of God filled the immense clarity of their eyes. They were poor Jews who were prohibited from having even an elementary education.

My grandparents Raquel and Abraham were born in Odessa and Sebastopol. My grandmother was an enchanting woman, with sleepy, almond-colored eyes. She wore black dresses, and in the early dawn would head to the factories in order to roll cigarettes with her amber-colored fingers. My grandfather was apprenticed to a tailor from the time he was eight years old, and worked at the home of some distant relatives who allowed him to sleep on the smallest table in the shop.

When Abraham turned seventeen, he married my grandmother Raquel, who was shy and beautiful. Her hands were slender and agile, like the fireflies in an Odessa evening. She rolled cigarettes as if they were velvet strips caressed by her luxuriant hands. Raquel was young, yet she sometimes thought about the fate of those bodies destined to suffer persecuted lives.

## Tools of the Trade

My grandfather was not allowed to study foreign languages or applied or theoretical sciences. He attended the rabbinical school in Odessa until he was eight years old. At that time, he learned about the art of silence and memorized certain Biblical passages so that he could always recite them in the solitude of his poverty.

My grandfather also learned the tailor's trade and grew

very fond of needles, thread, and remnants of cloth. Once he told us that years later, when he was in Turkey, unable to speak the language and looking for work, he would communicate his craft by placing a threaded needle in his mouth. The merchants understood him and employed him as a tailor's apprentice.

My father would use other tools: radioactive substances, luminous isotopes, and cobalt-colored test tubes. This is how he would earn his living as a doctor and later as a researcher of invisible things.

History assigns its values to the trades of these two men, father and son, but I think that both trades were fine and beautiful, clear like the unadorned light of all beginnings.

## Fortunes of War

My grandparents were poor working people and incapable of prospering because they were Jews. They had to live in certain districts so that people would not curse them or harm them. The only education permitted to them was that offered at the rabbinical school. This, however, did not prevent Tzar Nicholas from recruiting Jews into his armies for nearly twenty years.

My grandmother told me that during the First World War, when the soldiers were marched away, the women walked behind the men in a lethargic, confused, aching, and almost insane stupor until fatigue prevented them from following any further. The Russian countryside became filled with disemboweled shoes and dejected garments, making rubble out of human suffering.

It is said that the women followed behind the soldiers numb and broken, with death in their gaze. In just this way my grandmother Raquel, with her children, followed my grandfather Abraham for more than thirty kilometers.

As Raquel walked barefoot her eyes acquired the prophecies that accompany darkness, while her cheek-bones resembled a dry garden, numbed by terror. Behind the silence of the empty nights, the sounds of the breathless women could be heard. This is how my grandmother bid farewell to my grandfather in those opaque zones of war. But it was not his destiny to die.

My grandfather spoke very little about the deeds of war. His shyness seemed to deepen as he grew more silent through the years. That was his way of driving away evil omens and the ghosts of the fallen that appeared in the remote city of Odessa, stranded behind the mist.

During the war my grandfather began to stutter. When he crossed the Carpathian Mountains in 1915, he fell into a trench where he lay buried for one week. By a miraculous stroke of fate, he survived. After that incident, something happened to his speech, some-thing that made him measure his words and alternate them with the sounds of pain.

Abraham returned to Odessa in 1917 after three fierce and lost years of war. As my grandmother and he embraced, their bodies seemed like a cloud of vapor rising from the earth. Finally they would be able to walk along the shore again and make rings of love between their hands.

## The Wages of Fear

When the autumn brightness settled and the words grew thinner in the tenuous light of a leisurely late afternoon, I would approach my father and hold his hands with curiosity and love. I would grasp those hands and listen to the voice that had told me so many times that perhaps the God who was in heaven was even more upon on the earth. Only then I would ask my father to tell me about the dark bonfires of the pogroms that had been experienced by my grandparents before they left the Russia of Tzar Nicholas. My father, formally and with a distant tenderness in his words, told me that the Cossacks had burned the houses and had dragged my grandmother by the few strands of hair that remained on her head. While they burned the house, they amused themselves before the meager spoils of the Jews. "That is what the Cossacks did to your grandparents, daughter of my dreams," he said, and his voice grew as faint as the tenuous and fragile light that surrounded us.

Suddenly the darkness became thicker. The afternoon and night flowed together, confusing themselves before the smells of delicate fragrances, and my father, downcast, told me that this violence was not merely an evil aberration. The burning of the houses and the dragging of my grandmother by the hair were a denial of possibilities, a denial of education in its most fundamental sense. The violence could be traced to the pilgrimages of hate, and it was permanent, in all of its perfidious splendor. It always liked to keep all of its victims in suspense. It liked to forget them and forever leave them wandering, lost among the steep and solitary hills.

When I asked my father about the Cossacks, he would shiver and hug me, and the two of us would remain covered by a strange fright resembling secrets and explicable silences. In the distance I saw the flames engulfing my grandmother's house and her hair running between the hands of hate and terror.

## Istanbul

Because of the persecutions of White Russians and Jews, my grandfather decided to leave Odessa forever and move to Turkey in 1917. My grandmother did not pack any belongings because she did not possess any. Instead she carried a candle and a handful of salt and sugar so that she would never be without these three household essentials. She continued interpreting dreams, lighting candles, and opening windows while others closed their doors.

Journeys for Jews are like the textures of memory. More than wanderers, my grandparents were great navigators in cargo ships, sleeping on deck with the wealth of a blanket of stars and the rumblings of the sea. My grandparents reached Istanbul on foot without money or shelter. They lived among the dilapidated roofs of the city, among the wailing minarets and ruins of light.

Istanbul, at that time still called Constantinople, the city of ancient Byzantium, became the site of my grandparents' first exile. There they learned to speak Turkish and to love the marble games and street corner cafes. My grandfather always remembered the Turkish language, which would become so useful to him in Quillota, Chile, when he negotiated with the Arabs of the region, especially the Syrians and the Lebanese.

The story of the years in Turkey dissolves, rematerializes, and filters through certain scenes remembered by my father. For example, his parents were so severely poor that they did not have enough money to buy a table. My grandfather, with the meager funds that he had, bought a gray door from the owner of a nearby cemetery, which he then used as a table. Once one banana adorned the center of the table and was cut into five portions, becoming supper at nightfall for my grandparents and their three sons. My father's eldest brother, Manuel, had been born in Russia. Two more brothers, Rodolfo and Marcos, were born in Istanbul.

My father himself would be born in another land, at the end of another voyage.

## Mediterranean Reveries

I immerse myself in its contradictory calmness and in its texture and hue, which is bluer than a child's sky. I stand before the Mediterranean Sea, with its sailing boats and fragrances, its sailors intoxicated by hazelnuts and light. The light here is like a balloon that floats and quivers above this secret, fragile, and bold sea, which separates continents and lives, opening solitary frontiers in the stillness of its nights.

I like to look at this sea, which resembles no other, because here the fairy tale is simple. Every overturned rock on its shores tells a story and is the memory of other memories. This is the sea that continues inventing the disfiguration of all times, but it is still, nevertheless, seductive and transparent, a sea that transgresses the hearts of women who cry and love.

We are seated before its shores on a balcony overlooking its calm yet turbulent waters. This is a sea that bewitches through its ancient stones. This is the same sea that created a route for the disfigured navigators of exile. It is the same sea that my grandparents crossed on their journey from Istanbul to their next destination, Marseilles.

No one knows how long their voyage took or if they stopped in the night to hear the sea's echos and think about the wickedness of hatred, of intolerance, of war. Perhaps my grandmother stopped to listen to it and to pray. Perhaps then, within the arms of the sea, she remembered the doors of her house and looked for the thresholds where she might take refuge from the cold and the sadness.

What did the impoverished navigators do while they crossed the Mediterranean Sea? In what times and cities did my grandfather wander, thinking? I wonder if he searched among the shadows of the night for the garden of his house or the door of a burning synagogue.

This is the Mediterranean Sea, generous and cruel in its tides, anointing life and death, exiles and returns. My grandparents crossed this same sea that I contemplate today. The more I gaze upon its horizon, the more I lose myself in its timeless tides which show me that I, too, am a foreigner—a wanderer, an exile—who knows nothing about the cartography of returns. Like my grandparents, perhaps I look for a home, a synagogue smelling of moss.

## Marseilles

When they left Turkey behind, Raquel, Abraham, and their three young sons continued sailing along the Mediterranean until they came to France, where they disembarked at Marseilles and stayed for five years in the city that has always received immigrants from many continents.

My grandfather continued practicing his tailor's craft and my grandmother continued rolling cigarettes, and between the arduous work and the impossible dreams of a better future, my father was born. They gave him the Jewish name Moses because, just like the biblical Moses, he was born in a seaport. They first called my father little Moshka, then Moïse, then the Spanish Moisés, and finally Aggie.

I tell my father that he is a Provençal gentleman, true to the place of his birth, with aristocratic tastes. He is well-mannered and dignified in his passions and in the seasoning of his meals. We both know, however, that all Jews are part of a disinherited people.

In fact, my father was born in the public ward of a hospital for the indigent in Marseilles. Today he is a renowned international scientist, but he will always be a refugee, exiled from countries and from history.

In the seventies my parents decided to look for the dilapidated house where my father once lived and the hospital where he opened his eyes for the first time. The old neighborhoods had disappeared, and the only people living in them now were drug dealers and Moroccan immigrants lost in the silence of foreigners. The street where my father was born was sordid and abandoned, as poor in its way as it had been in the time when his mother and brothers waited for the tickets that would carry them to the South American continent.

## From Marseilles to Valparaíso

My grandfather had a brother, known as Don Marcos Agosín, who was also a tailor and had managed to establish a genuine textile empire in Valparaíso, Chile, on the other side of the planet from Marseilles. Marcos assured Abraham of a magnificent future in Chile, and on a sunny morning in 1923, my grandfather undertook his last sea journey. He embarked on a vessel in Marseilles bound for Valparaíso, leaving behind my grandmother, who waited for the tickets that would bring her to the new world.

His absence lasted three years. Women with mischievous tongues told Raquel that her good husband Abraham had abandoned her and that he would never send her the yearned-for tickets. My grandmother laughed to herself and sang some Russian melodies, not paying much attention to these women because above all else she loved Abraham. Finally, one afternoon, the tickets arrived. Raquel's eldest son, Marcos, recalls that he received them with so much emotion that he was almost run over by an automobile.

My grandmother, a determined and bold woman, embarked on a cargo ship bound for South America with my father and his three brothers. How is it possible to imagine that risky crossing toward hope or shadow?

My father says that his mother dressed him and his brothers in black, to blend in with the night, so that they would not be thrown overboard during the sicknesses in that interminable voyage across moving seas. My father did contract German measles, and his face was covered with spots, dimmed by the sadness of solitude and poverty. The sailors of the vessel wanted to toss him into the sea, thus fulfilling the prophecy of his name, but my grandmother hid him under her grey wool skirts for forty days until Moshka recovered from the illness and arrived at Valparaíso harbor blue and disheveled beneath the mist. When my grandmother arrived with her sons, faded and barefoot, Uncle Marcos greeted them at the dock. And it was here, in Chile, in the farthest corner of the planet, that she lived and died happy and grateful.

## My Father Saved from the Waters

My father arrived in Chile barefoot and vulnerable. His mother didn't wrap him up in yellow rags, but when they reached the immigration offices in the shabby port of Valparaíso, with its hills teeming with fireflies, they gave his name as Moses—in Spanish, Moisés. In Marseilles he had been called Moïse, and he was also known as little Moshka. My father still doesn't know exactly what his name is. He suffers from the universally interminable problems associated with identity and with baldness.

For me he is simply the father whom I love more than anything because he is eccentric, curt in his answers, fragile and transparent. I love his piano playing at dawn and I love him because he doesn't like to lie. He also assured me when I was six years old that God does not have wings.

This is the story of Moses, Moïse, Moshka, or Moisés,

because in addition to his having been saved from the waters, his repudiation of organized religion, and his passionate love for enzymes in flies, my father is truly an exceptional being.

## Starry Meadows

My father says that his parents never talked to him about the vicissitudes of life and the voyages they had made, even though his questions were endless. My grandmother, wide and generous, only said that in the middle of storms she would breathe deeply, very deeply, as if it were the end of the world, and then she would begin to sing. She sang when they crossed the Strait of Magellan with its greenish blizzards, and she wasn't afraid of being barefoot. When my grandmother first glimpsed the lights in the harbor of Valparaíso, she breathed deeply again and filled up with happiness and yellow flowers like a starry meadow.

## Valparaíso

Valparaíso, disorderly and confused, hanging from the highest transparency of air and light. It is a city shrouded by the wind, always singing and happy. Valparaíso, so beloved behind the fine misty rain of the early dawn. This is where the pirates came, where Francis Drake hid in his colorful home, where María Graham wrote her long diary about life in Chile, becoming the first Chilean writer of the nineteenth century, and where Rubén Darío wrote *Azul*. This is also where my paternal grandparents arrived after their long journey from Marseilles, and where my other grandfather arrived from Hamburg. Their blue ghosts still live in this city whipped by earthquakes and by the eccentricities of its inhabitants.

Valparaíso, I, too, love you, and in my dream-filled nights I sketch you with a great silvery moon and with the body of a laundress covered with smoke and rising toward the sky in all its vastness.

## Cities

At times I wish I could go to certain cities where my grandparents slept and dream in the nakedness of memory about places like Odessa, immersed in the liquid vapors of a succulent summer, or about Istanbul, with its veils and ancient garments, or about Valparaíso, with its maddening hills and meadows and its brides dreaming of love. Perhaps I would sleep in Chile's Central Valley or in Quillota, the city where my grandparents settled, next to the silky and oily texture of the avocado pears, the cherimoyas, and the imported clocks carrying the secret messages of thousands of voyages. At times I wish I could dream my grandparents' dreams, pronounce their secret prayers and hide their tattoos outlined by terror. At times I would like to travel alone, so that I could simply dream about the cities that they visited and remember what they forgot and what they left behind: the sepia-colored photographs, the things they were not able to come back to look for, the things they learned not to lament. At times I wish I could return simply to sleep in certain cities, to smell the jasmine and fill myself with love.

## My Grandfather, Abraham Agosín

My grandfather was a silent, extremely timid and gentle man. He was very frugal with his words and generous with his acts. Despite his timid nature, my grandfather tried to use words with genuine generosity. He possessed an assured gentleness without pretensions, a generosity that was like a luminous flame.

When he became a man of means, each time one of his machinists would marry, he would give her a brand new sewing machine and a gold needle newly imported from France, because he knew with that sewing machine and those colored spindles of thread, his workers would find food and happiness.

In Quillota, the city where he settled in Chile, some people called him "the Quillotano," which implied his austerity and provincialism. When he went out to visit neighboring places, he would say that he was "internationalizing" himself. My grandfather never spoke a word of Russian in Chile, but expressed himself with difficulty in a poor Castillian. He also learned to read but never learned to write well in Spanish.

Speaking in Russian was strictly forbidden, and it is only now that I understand why. So great was his need to integrate and not be treated completely as a foreigner that my grandfather chose to hide his Russian in the deepest, most secret and captive region of his memory.

Nevertheless, he never managed to overcome his position as an outsider, an exile. Every time some people saw him pass by in the streets, they would call him "the Turk," which, curiously, is the same epithet often used to describe Arabs.

But my grandfather won the respect of many of the residents of Quillota. He was admired as much by the very devout women as by the school gatekeepers and the monks. He was courteous and knew how to listen. When he turned eighty years old, they honored him by naming him an illustrious citizen of Quillota. My grandmother, on the day of the inauguration, wore a violet-colored dress, sang a beautiful Russian song, and said, "Now I can light the Sabbath candles."

## My Grandmother, Raquel Kankolsky Agosín

My grandmother glowed like a firefly in love with the light. She moved very quickly, which was probably due to the many times she had to flee other lands as a tear-drenched refugee. After traveling from the Ukraine to Turkey and then on to France, she finally came to rest in Quillota, Chile, where she kept track of her life in a tiny blue book. She wanted me to learn from these stories, which she wrote in Spanish but transliterated into Russian Cyrillic characters.

My grandmother was like a sage. Words but not laughter eluded her. She was like Bruria, the wife of a studious man named Rabbi Meir, who would listen to discussions of the Talmud in a back room; though she could never study the sacred scriptures directly, she somehow learned them. Like Bruria, my grandmother knew how to listen, and when the society ladies of Quillota's charitable institutions asked her if Jews had horns, she only smiled. When my grandfather ordered her not to make any further donations to the Jesuits or to the Hebrew school, she listened and laughed, and then took out her notebook, which was always next to her blue suitcase. My grandmother always had a suitcase filled with clothing under her bed. She also had a silk blouse and four pairs of shoes. She said that she was always ready to travel just in case.

My grandmother Raquel never told me anything about Odessa. All she ever said was that she liked to walk along the coast, arm in arm with my grandfather. She never spoke to me about the pogroms or the times that they would spit at her in the streets and shout "white, ugly Jew dog." She only told me that the Russians were great poets and that they drank tea with much sugar and passion.

When my grandmother spoke in Spanish she seemed to fill up with a warm transparency and pronounced her *rr*s and *ñ*s with splendor. Her voice was so melodic, as if she were singing and leaving the earthly life behind.

It was true that she wore mismatched shoes and was the most eccentric and exotic person in the small city of Quillota. She dressed all in black with a small violet-colored hat, black net stockings, and a pair of blue shoes. But among my grandmother's many virtues, the most extraordinary was that she knew how to sing in Russian, Turkish, and French. She had a beautiful soprano voice. When important dignitaries came to celebrate wakes and baptisms, they invited my grandmother to sing in three languages. They called her the three-colored lady and they would bow and curtsy to her, cloaked behind a veil of humility. She sang on and on; she reinvented songs and rewrote her history, pretending that she was a student of well-known Russian songmasters. She never told them that she had once had to sing beneath the pillows because Jews were not allowed to sing in public.

## Husband and Wife

My grandparents were like oil and vinegar, never like water for chocolate. My grandfather was taciturn and reserved in his speech, much like my father and his brothers. In the late afternoon my grandmother sang, recited Russian poetry, and drank tea, which she sprinkled with vanilla and sweetened with immense lumps of sugar. My grandfather was neat and tidy. My grandmother, on the other hand, mixed dark green with lilac, lavender

with seaweed, french fries with caviar, olive oil and perfumed water. This is how she lived, defying death.
They both died, nevertheless, on the same day of the
year—my grandfather on February 14, 1973, and my grandmother on February 14, 1978.

My grandparents never talked about religion or
covered the mirrors in days of mourning. They also
didn't go to synagogue, as if that sinister past of the
pogroms should be erased, and that part of their identity should be usurped. However, my parents got married in a synagogue and my grandparents died like Jews,
buried in the Jewish cemetery of the region. For my grandparents, God was an irate and less than noble being
because he had deprived them of their childhoods. He
was a God who obliged them to work at an early age
and to enter shadowy pathways of adulthood in a foreign country.

## God and My Grandfather

Amid the mist and beyond disjointed memory, I ask
myself what my grandfather must have done as he
entered heaven. Did he shake hands with a taciturn and
punitive God? Or did he perhaps recognize dead
friends, last glimpsed beyond the thresholds in their houses of ashes and twisting flames?

My grandfather, like my father, never talked about
God or organized religion. Quillota did not have (nor
will it ever have) a synagogue, but it would have been

possible to go to a house of worship in nearby Viña del
Mar. However, this never happened. My grandfather
Abraham never approached houses of prayer, even
though he had a predilection for charity and donated
generous quantities of clothing and money to the poor
tailors of the city, to the nuns, and to the Hebrew
school of Valparaíso, as well as to his own brother.

It was God who had deprived my grandfather of a
childhood filled with idleness and games. Instead of allow-
ing him to play chess and gamble, this God obliged him
to learn about the damp texture of cloth and to sleep
on freezing tables that seemed like the antechambers
of icy death. To this God he begged for the shade and
solace of home. It was this God who didn't hear him in
Odessa or in Istanbul or Marseilles, not even in the dreadful boat that brought him to the sparkling port of
Valparaíso. Nearly all of his relatives died, at the hands
of either the Cossacks or the Nazis.

In Quillota, Don Abraham Agosín was happy with
his wife Doña Raquel. Both of them loved the silence
of summer, the fragrance of the bougainvillaea shrubs,
and the plaza with its pretentious ladies. They liked to
speak French, Russian, Turkish, and Spanish and avoided remembering those times when the houses of Jews
burned like uninhabited flames of long hair. My grandparents survived among the clouds of smoke, travelling
in nocturnal trains of love and life, headed toward
uncertain futures. They were happy in the city of the
avocado pears, and more than anything they loved

listening to my father passionately play Mozart and recite verses from Verlaine, and seeing him earn his medical degree. They never forgot their Odessa origins, that one was a tailor and the other a cigarette-making apprentice, and that they had a son who was a doctor in the New World. But I do not think my Grandfather thanked God for this good fortune.

## Brothers

My father is the last known survivor of his generation. About his brothers there are many secrets, words left unspoken.

I remember an afternoon by the seaside in 1964. Along the coast, spring had begun to subtly emit its nameless and unspeakable fragrances. The meadows were filled with forget-me-nots and purple pansies, and the Chilean shoreline was an ocean of flowers. Behind the most concealed corners of the house, my mother looked for the lizards that foreshadowed good luck. But the lizards did not appear, and the rose bushes in the garden in front of the house violently dried up.

I remember my father sitting next to the fireplace reading his science fiction books that arrived from the other side of the Argentine cordillera. The peace and tranquility of this moment, however, was soon to be disturbed by a messenger riding on a bicycle as swift as the wind and the butterflies. Profiled on his young man's face was the incomprehensible grief so commonly associated with death. He came to tell us that Rodolfo, my father's younger brother was lying on his deathbed at an emergency room in Santiago. Responding to this unsettling news, my father withdrew deeply into himself, as if his heart had been transported to the most profound and perverse zones of memory, immersed in a forest of burning figures.

We knew so little about my father's brothers. This was perhaps the first time I heard him talk about Rodolfo with tenderness, in a voice that already intuited the inevitable. Only now, before death's threshold, did my father dare to pronounce his name, to talk about and to love him.

What were my uncles like? Where did they live? In what shadowy place in our family history did they and we abandon ourselves? I approach memory and ask my father about them. He tells me the story of the flight from Russia and the humiliating poverty in which my grandparents lived, which immersed them in a nomadic life among the shadows.

My father says that his eldest brother, Manuel, was strange and reticent, and that he has erased all memories surrounding his existence. Moisés was twelve years old when Manuel disappeared forever from the lives of his parents, Abraham and Raquel. This was the last time my father saw him. They say that Manuel sometimes was seen preaching like a Christian beggar in the most remote sections of Central Valley. Some also say they saw him working as a plumber. All this they say and don't say, and my father doesn't tell and doesn't speak, but rather censors himself in the most perfidious and anguished of silences.

Rodolfo, his youngest brother, was taciturn and bold, a great mathematical genius but also a prisoner of alcohol. He committed suicide one spring morning in Santiago, Chile, by jumping from the fourth floor of his apartment building. My father managed to see him before he died of his injuries at the dilapidated Red Cross clinic where the poor of my country go to die. My uncle kept saying: "The Russians are after me; the Russians are after me," and Moisés vaguely recalled the secrets of the houses boiling among the flames and the hatred.

How did my grandparents get here from Russia? Who gave them visas? How did they pass through so many countries? These were our secrets, and perhaps it was for this reason that so little was said about the Russian past under Tzar Nicholas, where they persecuted Jews, especially those who were poor and destitute like my grandparents.

Marcos, the only brother I met, was too Chilean for our taste. He hid his Judaism as if it were a secret and sacred wound, and became a Freemason. He preferred to assimilate and devote himself to women and wine. Marcos married a crazy anti-Semitic woman, who wandered about the city of Quillota blessing herself and wearing enormous crosses. When he died, his wife burned several family photographs, and our traditions and history were erased like pages of memory into ashes.

I have often wondered how my father saved himself from that wrenching nostalgia, that indefinite, nameless sadness that comes from the profound loss of loved ones. He tells me that his parents were marvelous beings because they conserved their faith in life, with all its impurities and tragedies. They continued to believe in a life that gleamed in the evening, that wasn't dark in the night, and that prepared itself to receive the new day.

## Kaddish

Belloto is located between Viña del Mar and Olmué, in the central part of Chile where the Aconcagua River joins the Pacific Ocean and where the winter and summer evenings hold a breeze that is placid and calm, as if composed of bulrushes and transparent light. Life and death and the intermittent regions of repose do not contradict each other there. Belloto is a rural town, where men filled with solitude and wine usually rest beneath the shade of immense cypress trees. It is also the home of the only Jewish cemetery in Chile.

On all of my return trips to Chile, I visit my dead grandparents, who are near the entrance of the cemetery, as if they were leading a pilgrimage of the dead. Here also is the tomb of my cousin, Marcos Agosín, who died in the vastness of the sky in a parachuting accident. The graves are filled with stones, faithful to Jewish burial rites.

I enter through the door on the left side, which is how one gets to the house of the dead, and this is where my grandparents are: Abraham and Raquel, in their cool and melodious state. I like to approach their tombs and leave them little stones, following the tradition of the Jews of the desert, the Jews of Moses's time, who piled their grave sites with stones because the savage animals would rob the graves and grow by devouring the hearts of the dead.

I approach my grandparents in the early, shadowy light of day and the herons take to the air; the atmosphere is permeated with the smell of hyacinths and eucalyptus trees. The entire sky seems at rest because even the clouds are still, and the woman who cares for the dead tells me that they are napping. She recognizes me and says, "You are the daughter of Don Moisés Agosín, the son of Don Abraham. You have the same watery eyes and the same gaze." I like to be recognized. I like it when she names us, because through all the exiles, the borrowed and betrayed languages, we have lost our names. She tells me that I am from here, and it gladdens me that this guardian of the dead assures me that I belong somewhere.

I think of the prayers of the dead, the Kaddish lament that is like a deafening cry, a chant that drags us and splits us apart, reaching down into the most secret and hidden cavity of the soul. More than these prayers, death is perhaps well-timed and elegant. She arrives at the precise moment, between the opacity of all the mist and dissolving light. She comes and we follow her like obedient figures. Relieved, we accompany the messenger angels and depart without leaving a trace, only the names of who we were, the illusion of what we gave, with our hands extended toward the thresholds.

The graves of Jews are not filled with flowers, but instead with tarnished stones. When burying their beloved, the family members cast dirt upon their new resting places. I have seen my grandmothers drag themselves toward these graves frayed by tears, but relief seems to come quickly after they have cast the first handful. The earth is very fresh and cool. It fits into the hands of these women like precious gifts of love. Often I have seen them throw dirt on the grave while the men pray and a fine drizzle falls as if the sky itself were crying.

As a girl I always knew that this land tasted of hyacinths and lilacs, that it was composed of fragrant aromas and glittering grass. These were the burials that I imagined as a child and did not attend. Sometimes in the secret alcoves of the long night I listen to the Kaddish prayers and to my grandmothers covering their husbands as the trees modulate the voice of the praying rabbi covered with a white shawl.

The cemeteries of my country are dilapidated and plaintive. It seems as if the wind itself darkens beyond the crevices and that the porticos of the doors take on the smells of pestilence and solitude.

My grandfather Abraham's life ended in a hospital near the central plaza in Quillota. His heart stopped

beating in 1973, the historic year when Salvador
Allende was at the height of his popularity and could
still count on the support of the nation, especially the
young intellectuals. Since he was a socialist president,
the United States, that great and merciless country to
the north, declared an embargo on the exportation of
medicines to Chile, an embargo just like the one being
applied to Cuba today. My grandfather Abraham, who
hung chocolates from the trees and spoke Turkish,
Russian, and Spanish, perished because of a lack of oxy-
gen, medicine, and bandages. He died without knowing about the dictatorship that would soon come to
Chile–about the burning of Chilean books and the persecution that would have reminded him of his Russian
birthplace.

When my grandfather died my father cried tears of
anger, and five years later, on the same day of the year,
my grandmother Raquel, the mother of little Moshka,
also died, alone in her house in Quillota, surrounded
by the aromas of her samovar.

Today my grandparents are buried in the small
Jewish cemetery, where they lie beneath the swallows
and the almond trees and are under the good care of
the graveyard keepers who are in charge of feeding the
tombs and talking with the dead.

In the city of the dead I realize that I will never be
able to leave Chile. Even if they blindfolded my eyes,
I would return to her lap, to her afternoons and the cool
dreams of her dead.

I withdraw from the cemetery and return through the door on the right, which faces the road of the living. The tomb offers peace and a strange happiness that derives from sharing a meal with the dead and cleaning their orchards. Following an old Talmudic custom, I wash my hands and cross the hill of the living.

# QUILLOTA

## City of Churches and Avocados

1926–1939

## Blue Suitcases

When my grandparents crossed dark, sloping roads and ivy-entwined forests, they always brought along for the journey a candle, some salt, and two or three photographs in order to talk with the dead. All their possessions, their beloved objects, remained behind at the mercy of a furious, outraged destiny. However, those photographs of my great grandparents came to occupy a central place in the living room of the house in Quillota. Sometimes my grandmother would contemplate them from a distance. In one photograph, the family stands in a garden by the sea, looking happy. I gaze at them, wanting to know more, wanting to ask them where the rest of the family was, what they did during reunions, how they wore their hair, and what my uncles talked about.

I grew up with these photographs, which were placed in different areas of the house, until one day they disappeared into my aging grandmother's blue suitcase. She put them there because this way she would be prepared to undertake another pilgrimage and flee amid the drizzling sorrow of another cloud-filled night.

## A Jewish Christmas

My grandfather's brother Marcos, the one who brought him from Marseilles, was a real magnate despite his humble beginnings. When he arrived in Chile he installed his tailor shop beneath a faded blue umbrella.

As the years passed, my great uncle Marcos managed to establish a great fortune. He had automobiles with chauffeurs, homes at the beach, and a principal residence in Valparaíso on the aristocratic Polanco Palace Hill. However, misfortune strangled his guardian angel and he lost everything in nights of gambling and love.

My grandfather Abraham decided to begin a new life in Quillota, the city of avocado pears, cherimoyas, and sun, located some seventy kilometers from Valparaíso in the rich valley of the Aconcagua River. In order to reach Quillota it is necessary to pass through tiny villages filled with blue and lilac meadows, villages filled with the dust of abandonment, where life is reserved and slow.

My grandparents, assisted by Uncle Marcos, established themselves in Quillota with great dignity and great poverty. My grandfather dedicated himself to fulfilling the trade of his ancestors. He was generous and noble. Every year he would give the nuns of the town some dark-colored fabrics for their habits. He was loved by the people in the town, who once commissioned him to decorate the city with stars for the Christmas festivities. Since five-pointed stars were aesthetically difficult to make, my grandfather made six-pointed stars instead, and on Christmas Eve, the entire city of Quillota was inhabited with glorious golden Stars of David. The city was Jewish for the night and no one knew it.

## Illustrious Citizens

As in all small cities, life in Quillota pulsated in the square, where the people converged for late afternoon strolls. Rich as well as poor would acknowledge each other respectfully, and the most wealthy would take off their hats with the subtle elegance of the false provincial aristocracy. Quillota had its illustrious citizens: the mayor, the chief of police, the chief of the fireman's club, and the director of the boys' school. These illustrious bald-headed and big-bellied men decided who would enter the private clubs and prestigious schools, with their high-class names. The principal clubs in the city were those of the Germans and the Masons. Citizens who did not belong to these clubs were branded as communists, imposters, and poorly dressed and shabby eccentrics. My grandparents were not able to enter either the Masonic or the German Club, but this didn't worry them much because they were used to being outsiders at all times.

The city was filled with churches. It even had a cathedral, which was leveled in one of the earthquakes and remained unbuilt for want of a pious soul able to collect sufficient money to reconstruct it.

The Salesian priests, who were powerful and perverse in their hositilities and prejudices, told my father that it was unfortunate that a Jew was such a good student. Now I believe that he has come to pardon and even poke a little fun at those anachronistic and racist priests, who used to sunbathe nude on the rooftops of the monasteries.

## Cemeteries

As a young boy my father lived near the cemetery. When my father's parents moved to Quillota they rented a dark wooden house on Móyaca Hill, which in Mapuche means "the frozen breast of a woman." He liked the hill, and would wander among the rocky crests of the living and the dead. This explains his predilection for bones and skeletons, but more than anything, it explains that vast silence that covers him like a shroud of stories yet to be told.

My father's early childhood in Quillota was spent in this small, dilapidated house with a damp and sometimes muddy floor. Because the house was near the cemetery, he learned to talk with the dead and to bring them beverages and offerings, like a faithful follower of pre-Columbian traditions, even though he was a Jewish child from Marseilles. However, he knew then that the dead need the sweet companionship of children, and it was among them that he found his first playmates and tranquility. For him, tombs represented a permanent presence of rubble and humanity.

## A Vulnerable Childhood

When my paternal grandparents, Abraham and Raquel, came to Quillota, they decided not to celebrate either Jewish or Christian holidays so as to not call attention to their different traditions and beliefs. Sometimes my grandmother would close the windows of her three-story house and cover them with wrapping paper, then light the candles on Fridays. She would also play Russian marches and drink from a samovar that was not imported from Russia but bought instead from some poor gypsies who came to Quillota thirsty and looking for shelter.

My grandparents were the first Jewish family that lived in Quillota. At first the community didn't know how to treat them and chose to disregard them, leaving them alone and at peace. The inhabitants of this small town had fewer prejudices than those of the big cities. My grandfather was a friend of a priest. They talked every afternoon while drinking an exquisite red wine and they discussed evolution and the impossibility of the soul's absolute kindness.

Individuals shouted "Jew-boy" at my father when he crossed the village square and when he returned home downhearted about not being able to play tennis and soccer and about being too mild-mannered for a basketball player. Years later, when he lived in Santiago as an established doctor, his height and Jewishness also prevented him from joining certain established institutions. Nevertheless, he transformed all of the rancor of his past into a silent and deliberate love, an astute and pious understanding toward the ignorant. This is why my father later chose to send his daughters to the Hebrew Institute, a private Jewish school in Santiago. He simply wanted us to have a clear sense of our identity and to know what it means to be Jewish. He wanted us to know our history and to know how to defend ourselves, and he did not want us to hear ever again the songs sung in all of the schools in Chile, "Who ate all the bread in the oven?" and the chorus responding, "The Jewish dogs, the Jewish dogs." He never wanted us to hear the priests at catechism chanting, "Who killed Jesus?" and the choir responding, "The Jews killed Jesus. The Jews killed Jesus."

## School Days

My father was not permitted to attend private parochial schools, so he was educated in Quillota's public school, a modest and gentle provincial school. He received a magnificent education, with great music teachers who would play the violin barefoot during recess. He learned to speak French and English fluently at a young age because the teaching of foreign languages was an essential part of the curriculum in Chile.

Despite all of these benefits, my father's school also reflected the values of the time in Chilean society—Victorian and above all conservative Catholic values,

such as the condemnation of relationships with the oppo-
site sex. My father tells of the episode of a Romeo who
was found holding hands with his sixteen-year-old
Juliet, who had two bunches of poppies tied in her hair.
The following morning the principal expelled the two
students from school in a public ceremony; this is
how a beautiful gesture of love like a ring, like a sweet
passion, was punished before the astonished students,
among whom was my father.

Almost forty years later a savage dictatorship
appeared, which, like the principal, condemned the happiness of adolescence, the beauty of a first kiss, long hair,
and books of poetry. And again the young people
searched for hidden foliage where they could run
around barefoot and idle and kiss each other in the parks.

In Quillota, my father was the only Jewish student
in the entire public school system. While in school he
experienced that strong pro-German influence and
growing anti-Semitism that could already be perceived
long before the war. During a bakers' strike, students
chanted in the school choruses that the Jews had eaten
all of the bread in the oven. I think it was from that time
that my father, who had such a tenuous identity, understood the avatars of fate and what it meant to be called
a Jew.

Nevertheless, he had exceptional teachers like
Francisco Torres, who practically adopted him in order
to teach him good table manners. My father went to visit
him in the afternoons after school, and together they

would drink delicious late-afternoon tea and my father would learn how to hold a fork and knife correctly and to enjoy the delightful thickness of the butter and to believe in men of good faith.

## Taking Notes

All of my father's education, including his time at the university, was characterized by a great absence of texts, since books were expensive and difficult to get. He studied by means of notes that were loaned or paid for, and in this precarious way he learned and memorized. Sometimes certain powerful friends of my grandfather would bring my father books as gifts from their trips abroad. My father would think about the abundance of books in the marvellous libraries of the United States.

## Escutti High School

My father completed his high school studies at the Santiago Escutti Orrego School in Quillota, which is today the site of a greengrocer's shop. It was the end of the 1930s, and the atmosphere of the times was tense and sinister. Almost all of the city supported the Third Reich because of the limited yet powerful German minority of southern Chile, who also owned land and country estates in areas of the Central Valley, not far from Quillota.

Chile at that time was a profoundly pro-German nation. This was reflected in the German-style coffeehouses that existed throughout the country as well as in the exaggerated emphasis placed upon kuchens and the best recipes for wurst. The German Club still exists in the city. At that time it was in its heyday, and in the evenings it was filled by men in dark uniforms who did not conform to the cool air of Quillota nights. In the streets they constantly harassed my father, telling him that his life would end since the victorious German troops were advancing and the only acceptable race was the Aryan race, which would reign in Chile. Professors like Señor Benigno Islas and Señor Rodríquez, who were especially fond of my father, protected and accompanied him with the subtlety of love during those dangerous and wrenching years. Chile—frail, narrow, and beautiful—seemed to have succumbed as an accomplice to a pro-Germanic history. Years later, in 1973, this history would palpitate within its own flesh under Pinochet's fascism.

Despite these historical forces—or, perhaps, because of them, in that small provincial school my father had the opportunity to learn important lessons, like the one about true piety residing in a tolerant soul. He forgave the Salesian fathers who grew indignant before his successes, as well as the young students of the German schools who marched through the square bearing portraits of Hitler. He also remembered the beloved teachers, the conversations at teatime, and the wind of the

Central Valley caressing his skin. Likewise he remembered Freud and Jung, the great epic poems of Spain, France, and England, and above all the humility and delirium of Don Quijote.

Years later, when my father married and received his degree in medicine, the first professor he invited to his home was the friendly man who had taught him to converse over a cup of tea and never to put his hands in his pockets. But my father remembers other professors who were deep anti-Semites. Although they never told him directly that they didn't wish to teach him because he was a Jew, my father was wise enough to realize that this was the case—especially when they gathered in secret meetings to plan the glorious future of the Third Reich.

Because my father's studies coincided with the rising Nazism that permeated this remote country in South America, he had very few friends at school. During recess he could hear people talk about how soon the Jewish race would be eliminated, and how he would be among those who would perish. Emilio Videla was my father's best friend. He was the son of the gym teacher, and years later he died of typhoid, as did Luchito, the school janitor, who would give my father chicken sandwiches for good memory and raisins to revive lost loves. My grandfather would give him beautiful blue suits with green jackets.

# Willi

He had the gaze of someone gone speechless, of those displaced beings who lose the capacity to experience wonder and love. He told me that his name was Willi and that he was from Quillota, my father's city. His words interwove with themselves, as if he wished to leave behind secret signs and forge alliances. He told me that during Pinochet's terror, they had tortured him beyond pain and humiliation, and that his brother, overcome by dementia, had killed twenty-three boys in Quillota and also denounced him. He told me this while I imagined those men decapitated in peaceful Quillota, the city which sheltered my grandmother and let her sing songs in Russian, Turkish, French, and sometimes in Spanish.

The conversation continued, dampened by all the subtle cadences of those who have suffered, until he told me that he knew my father through his father, the legendary Alejo. Alejo was the illustrious doorman of the high school in Quillota, advisor, pimp, enlightened procurer, and above all a vendor of egg bread for memory, eggplants for love, avocados to fatten the ankles, and garlic to frighten away evil spirits and the dead. Willi was the son of Alejo, who sometimes fulfilled the roles of minister, secretary, prophet, and faithful advisor of secondary education. Willi tells me that Alejo was ninety-one years old when he died and that for his burial on the hill in Móyoca, he was accompanied by forty-two taxis, four buses with women's names, and a thousand former students, among them senators and vineyard owners, as well as the children of Quillota, who continued eating egg bread to recover lost memory, eggplants to invent love, and sandwiches, Alejo style, in order to warm the soul and recover happiness.

## Sundays in Quillota

On Sundays, during my childhood, we prepared to go to our grandparents' house. My mother always chose colorful dresses for us to wear and tied our hair with red ribbons. We travelled from Santiago to Quillota, and even though the trip only took two hours, it seemed like an eternity to us. My sister and I spent the time counting rocks and small pebbles like the prisoners who tidied up the roads, and we felt an enormous agony for those who wasted their liberty.

When we reached Quillota my father became silent. I think it is because he wished to talk with the dead and because he needed to be prudent with his words. Then suddenly my grandfather Abraham would appear with a luminous smile. He wore green wool pants and a tape measure around his neck and would invite us to go out to the yard because there he would hang caramel sweets and colorful ribbons from the lemon trees. This is how many of our Sundays were spent, with trips from the city to the province, with the clock, the samovar, the balalaika, and the diaspora.

On Sundays we went to Quillota, full of hope, as if we were on an excursion to the oldest and deepest clearing of the forest. We liked to feel that insinuating and delicate aroma of peaches, loquats and cherimoyas on our skin. We also liked to sit alone in the square while the devout women, like eternal birds of mourning, emerged from the fifty-seven churches of the city, and we Jews, peaceful and surrounded by an aura of foreignness, watched them as a few widows looked at us disdainfully and said profane things that had nothing to do with the sweet ceremonies of God.

This is where my father grew up. On Sundays he felt even more lonely and uninhabited than usual as the muffled church bells seemed to announce the end of the world while all the diligent believers went to eight o'clock mass. My father watched them from a distance, next to the fountain in the square, while the light laced through the willow tree.

## My Grandparents' Home

When my father was ten years old and the family had begun to prosper, they left behind their little house near the cemetery and moved to a house at Freire 52 in downtown Quillota. My grandparents lived, worked, and died in this house.

Entering my grandparents' home was like approaching miraculous zones where memories filter through the intermittent dominions of dream. When we knocked on the heavy mahogany doors, a smell of lavender and ground nuts filtered down the stairs, as did the perfume of the eucalyptus branches that my grandmother used to fan herself and frighten away the bad spirits of Tzar Nicholas. She also hung a braid of garlic at the front entrance in order to ward off envy and evil omens.

We quickly climbed the steps of that house damaged by earthquakes, and my grandmother Raquel greeted us, laughing heartily and holding a sprig of oregano, garlic cloves, and a huge ball of chocolate that brought us closer to happiness. She was golden, like the fairies in books for rich little girls, but she was ours to play with. We could even dress up in her shoes.

Once we were settled in the austere room that held the samovar, she asked us to be silent. She would then begin to sing old Russian melodies at the piano and tell us that this is how she prayed to her ancestors, to the dead and to those who could not dance. When she finished her song or her weeping, she would open the windows of the disorderly house to drive away the dark rags of death and let the sunset penetrate the miraculous zone of memory.

## My Grandparents' Garden

In the summer, when the light stretched out like a timid bride covered with orchids, and the afternoon drew near, we visited my grandparents' home. We spent many lost and happy hours next to the leafy tree that covered us with fragrances and prophecies. In silence my grandfather generously cared for his avocado pears and cherimoyas.

Behind the house on a high terrace was a church and a small, almost secret convent. From below we fascinated ourselves observing the comings and goings of nuns and priests through the secret rooms, through those scary spaces where Jews would never be allowed to enter. I imagined the nuns and priests contemplating us through the bars from the silent, dark, and distant world of their cells.

Among all of the gardens I have known, I always return to my grandfather's, with its delightful summer aromas, its blindfolded priests and nuns, and the dark rituals of a shadowy love, and there I pray for peace and for the evanescent time of faith.

## The Samovar

Among all of my grandmother's possessions, I remember that noble and obstinate samovar that was bought from some dancing gypsies that were passing through the city of Quillota. It rested upon a tall piece of antique furniture—light and happy, participating in ceremonies of love and sorrow. To us it seemed to come from unknown territories, those dominions where my grandparents left behind their language and their legends. The samovar continues to remind me of fables from faraway lands and lost voyages.

## The Clock

In my grandfather's house stood the clock bought with his first tailor's paycheck. It was such a dignified, antique, and beloved clock. Abraham Agosín would wind it delicately with the wisdom of those who reach the maturity of old age, a time of serenity, filled with the peace of sages.

My grandfather approached the clock each hour and it seemed as if it carried the rhythms of memory and chance on his shoulders, changing the sounds that filtered through the rooms. Those days were beautiful; the clock's ticking was like God's winds resting upon his heart.

## Happiness

My father would sometimes ask himself if his parents were happy in that placid and provincial city of Quillota. He thinks that, in spite of my grandfather's austerity with spoken language and the frugality of his gestures, he was a judicious man who was loved by his friends and above all by those of the Arab colony, with whom he shared an infinite number of stories and alliances.

My grandparents were greeted with respect on their morning walks through that warm and majestic city square. They surely thought of Odessa, the rare visits to St. Petersburg, the lost shadows of so many voyages in the remote obscurity of clandestine boats. Nevertheless, they were happy and managed to learn Spanish and not speak in the language of their past.

## The Tribulations of Memory

Quaint and sunny Quillota. Diurnal Quillota, with your village square, games, balloon-filled Sundays, and my father strolling with his parents like a foreigner who contemplates himself and recognizes a detached and lonely figure in a less than hospitable world.

Idle and tranquil Quillota, with senior citizens stretched out on the ancient benches of your majestic and drowsy plaza. City of feudal landlords and ignorant soldiers who played at being powerful mayors dressed in dark suits. Ancient and forgetful city with subtle prejudices. As my father left school he heard them shouting, "Jew," "Jew," and at first he didn't know why.

My father was a good student but would not take notes because he believed that in order to outline the affairs of memory all one needed was to listen with care. He insisted that it served no purpose to keep promises written on paper or to write love letters on white napkins. My father was always an eccentric and solitary soul, disobedient and subversive, a faithful enemy of eggplants.

## Leaving Quillota

Provincial life, with its apparently peaceful comings and goings of gentlemen and ladies with bags of bread and almonds, ultimately became intolerable for my father. When he graduated from high school in 1939, Chile was definitively pro-German and fascist. The charisma of Hitler and strong signs of nationalism swept through the country, seducing many. Marrying a young German girl would bring one a step closer to achieving racial superiority. In school there were parades convened for defending the Third Reich and my father was told that soon there would be nothing left of him. This is why he moved to Santiago sometime in 1940.

He left Quillota with its lemon trees and gardens filled with rosy-cheeked girls, and in Santiago, at the university, he once again found himself in the position of being one of the few Jewish students. At that time Jews were not seen as appropriate students of medicine. They were considered part of a sinister mafia. Entrance to the Catholic university was forbidden to them. The University of Chile, with its dilapidated buildings, turned out to be more noble. However, even there, the prejudice of others marked him like the tattoos of the European concentration camps.

## My Father's City

I walk through my father's city, a city of the dead and the living. No one and nothing remains from his family. The names of our relatives seem to have endured only on that list of travelers who emigrated beyond the annihilated mirror of their own dreams.

## A Homecoming in Quillota

After almost twenty years away, my family returns to Quillota for a visit. The road is winding and beautiful along the way. In the distance appear meadows filled with flowers resembling bells or dresses of women in love, which sway in the melodious wind. Great expanses of land emerge with their immutable and generous trees, the pines and the willows, and the small rivers, the stone houses and a road that clears and darkens, dense with moss and birds that brighten the heaven's nearby path. This is the Central Valley of my country, where the land is fertile in avocados and the cherimoyas are huge and succulent.

When we reach Quillota, it is Sunday, and the square fills up with balloons and indigent women who dream of being someone else. German and Masonic clubs still exist there as well as clubs formed by members of old radical parties, by Socialists and a few Republicans of the Spanish Civil War, who dream of utopias.

My father murmurs that nothing has changed, save the disappearance of a few churches—not because of the absence of faith but because of earthquakes. As I walk beside my father, time seems to recede, and I imagine him with my grandparents, speaking Spanish with their heavy accents, erasing traces of the past. Emigrants carry with them the stigma of solitude and melancholy, of returning to towns to which one always returns.

My father smiles and I feel that he forgives the fact

that people look at him strangely and with a pity that judges. Now he is a successful man, and this is perhaps why the men of the German Club pardon him and greet him as he passes by. He is the only survivor of an ancestral line of wanderers.

*My father, Moisés Agosín, in Chile at about age five, dressed as a Russian soldier.*

*My father's father, Abraham Agosín, 1937.*

*My father's parents, Raquel and Abraham Agosín, in the late 1940s in Santiago de Chile.*

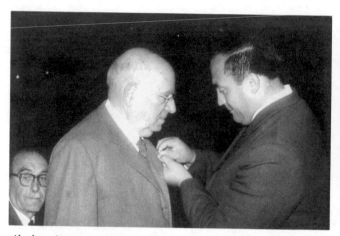

*Abraham Agosín receiving the Medalla de Honor in 1969 from the Town Hall of the city of Quillota for his contributions to the community.*

*My parents, Frida Halpern and Moisés Agosín, on their wedding day,
19 June 1948, at the Hotel Crillon in Santiago.*

*My father in the lab at the University of Chile in Santiago.*

# THE ARPEGGIOS OF MEMORY

## A Melodious Childhood

My father was nurtured by sounds in childhood. Music populated his cautious silence and enraptured him with sacred rhythms, and this is how he managed to reach the soul's peaceful chamber and free himself from the perfidious insinuations of his classmates, who despised him for being a Jew. Music calmed the anguish of his soul, brought him closer to the language of repose and helped him confuse the days with the nights. My father never collected stamps or coins, only Schumann and Mozart and the seeds of sound, marking his return to all of the imaginary houses where he always felt like a foreigner.

## Musical Gatherings

My father began his music classes in the city of Quillota. In the provincial high school, the musical gatherings and Miss Olea's music appreciation classes were legendary. The boys were eager to recognize the rhapsodies of Liszt and the heart-rending and terrifying symphonies of Beethoven. They also sang Verdi's operas, especially *Aida*.

My father also tells me that Miss Olea played Liszt as if she were seducing God, but that like all good Chilean women, she also knew how to sing and to dance the *cueca* with the passion of her ancestors.

Music went beyond the prejudices of creed and color and class. On Friday nights, the city of Quillota filled with the sounds of arpeggios and sonatinas. Everyone came to listen, even the poor children from the area next to the cemetery, who also recognized Liszt.

Later, my father scattered his talent among the small towns of the Central Valley, where they hired him to play in the silent movie houses when they showed films about gauchos. Many girls of the province dressed in lace in order to watch the young and delirious Agosín unleash his anguished soul before the keyboard, especially during scenes in which Apaches bound and gagged white men or cowboys kidnapped beautiful Indian princesses.

## Music Lessons

When he settled in Santiago, my father studied at the School of Modern Music, which I would also attend twenty years later. His teacher in Santiago was the distinguished René Amengual, a noble and strict guide who hated virtuosos and performers with long hands. Professor Amengual preferred small hands for interpreting Mozart, the warm and sweet hands of less pretentious performers.

Although he didn't like the drama of Beethoven, my father loved above all else the crystalline quality and warmth of Mozart and the dignity of Bach. He learned that it wasn't necessary to have heroic, long fingers in order to move about on the keyboard, and with time music began to accommodate itself to his humble soul.

## The Alchemy of Sounds

My father, in love with the melodious and the beautiful, with music that was crystalline and unpretentious, always wanted to be a pianist. His mother, concerned with economics, advised him to pursue a medical career. For many years he studied the false laws of alchemy, the philosopher's stone, the levitation of metal, and the metabolism of insects, although he continued dreaming about Mozart and Stravinsky, about the wild and passing music of birds.

For my father, music ran parallel to his medical studies. In the evening, when the city filled with cool night air and insomnia, he would sit at the piano. The women in the neighborhood would open their windows and the streets would fill up with the smells of chestnut and almond blossoms while my father played Mozart.

## The Piano

Ever since I was a young girl, the piano, which always stood in the main room of our home, was like a woman filled with sweet melodies. The piano was also like a hurricane and a wail. Instead of reading fairy tales and riddles, my father would calm his spirit and our bad childhood dreams by playing the piano, and we would keep perfectly silent, respecting those melodies that seemed to fly away from his hands like a breeze, like a piece of velvet on feast days.

At times, on perfidious nights of fear, when all of the uninhabited homes of exile would appear in our dreams, there stood the ceremonial and benign piano, as if it were waiting for our return, as if it had arrived with a flight of blue doves.

The piano was my father's companion. When he moved to my grandmother's boarding house in Santiago, which is where he met my mother, my father would play the piano loudly and with much ostentation until very early in the morning. He loved Mozart and Schubert, but was ordered to leave with his piano because of his eccentric habit of playing before the moon and the stars and waking up the neighbors. When he left he said, "Today I take the piano, but tomorrow I will come back for your daughter." My parents eventually married, but many years passed before they could afford a new piano.

In the first years after my father earned his medical degree, he had two dreams: to possess a baby grand and not to live near a meat packaging plant so that he would not have to hear the sound of flies and smell the odor of burnt meat. When he began to treat patients with more complicated and elegant illnesses, since he never charged for the common cold, he decided to buy a beautiful baby grand, a Steinway. He soon discovered, however, that his meager doctor's salary would not pay for such luxuries. He went to the bank, and when they learned that he was a doctor and not a pianist, they denied him a loan. He had to make do with a delicate English spinet, which he paid for in ten monthly installments over ten years.

That piano became a part of our afternoons. My sister Cynthia and I caressed the keyboard as we practiced scales, the sweet nocturnes and languid and crystalline Mozart pieces. Like my father, I studied at the prestigious School of Modern Music in Santiago, although I must confess that my great fantasy was to eat the bread with avocado pear jelly that they sold in the cafeteria. I had a difficult time reading the notes and Ms. Fabiola asked me if I was myopic. "No," I said, "I'm an Agosín."

## The Baby Grand

When we came to the United States, all we had in the otherwise empty living room was an immense baby grand piano. My father had purchased the piano hoping that the music would diminish the sadness of emigration. No one visited us, and the suspicious neighbors received us at their doors without letting us cross their thresholds.

My father consoled us with Chopin and Beethoven. He told us to get used to the possible insults because these would remind us of the voyages that his parents had undergone with a sack of bread on their shoulder, a little salt and sugar in their pockets, and the candles for Fridays.

## Songs

My father is not an observant Jew. His Judaism is revealed in his meditative attitude before the vicissitudes of life, in his respect for others, and in his sense of gratitude toward human beings in general. Although he would not go to synagogue with us, on holidays he would tell us that faith and prayer relieved the soul and that among the habitual sobs of the Jewish people, it was always wonderful to be able to sing.

On the way to the temple on Portugal Street in Santiago, we and our grandparents would walk through stone paved streets and flowery gardens where students would hold hands and kiss in the innocence of their adolescence. This is where the German Jews went because, curiously, synagogues in Chile were segregated into Ashkenazim and Sephardim. The Sephardim were happier than the austere Ashkenazim, but somehow all of them sang and rocked among the melodies that caressed their souls. More than a race or nation, we Jews are a people of song.

## Keyboards and Dancing Numbers

When my grandmother Raquel was seventy years old she decided to study accounting to help organize her world and to make more sense out of the numbers that danced in her head so that she would be less excessive in her donations to the dead and the living. Raquel also decided to study piano so that she could understand why her son Moses loved Mozart and played those sonatas as if he were immersed in a dream beneath a flowering tree.

I recall how, with her cigarette-rolling hands, she tried to cross the shores of the piano as if she were crossing rivulets of water and were thinking of those rivers in Odessa and the seacoast at Marseilles. Perhaps in her delirium, she also thought about the domes of Istanbul, the misty docks of Valparaíso. My grandmother Raquel loved life, with french fries scattered on the dilapidated kitchen floor. She loved laughter without boundaries like a waterfall, a solitary whistle between ships. She also collected matched and unmatched pairs of shoes.

Together with her piano lessons, she decided to write a memoir and thus recorded the things in her life, like home movies, stories about the nuns on the corner, a Turkish poem, and many songs in Russian and Spanish, as well as love's hard knocks. She was a poet who, after leaving behind the pogroms and the cigarette factories, became a faithful collector of shoes, fireflies, butterflies, and of extravagant donations for the barefoot children of Quillota, the anti-Semitic nuns, and

the beggars. She played the piano like someone touch
ing an essence, the rhythms of fleeting happiness, and
she was swept up in a whirling and melodious wind.

## Lost Objects

I dream about Odessa, about my grandparents holding
hands, united by rings of smoke spreading out over the
Black Sea. I dream about them in their fleeting cross
ings in the night, like lost assassins dispossessed of
their faces, their faith, and their cities. Between dreams
someone shaves my hair, silences and undresses me, and
I whisper to him that I must travel, cross walls, and return
to the time of my grandparents and of those diluted and
diffused generations. I awaken angry and, still half-dream
ing, I ask: Why do they take away our clothes and shave
off our hair? Why do they decapitate us? I ask them
at least, to let me buy flowers for the graves of my loved
ones, and between the dreams, beyond wakefulness, some
one tells me: We have found the balalaika. We have found
the balalaika.

## Eva

It was dusk, the time of the deep silences, of the refuge
within obscurity. My father prepared to play the piano.
When he played he was essentially alone, as if the
sounds of that resonating music were part of him, con
necting him to the universe beyond that magical sphere

of the room where we were all gathered—his children, his wife—and to the evanescence and eternity of life fusing together. That night, for the first time, he said that he wanted to tell me a love story, so I approached him, wanting to listen patiently and with happiness. I wanted to be the best listener so that I could rescue all of his tenderness and I wanted to be the best child, the most faithful recipient of his story.

He told me about a virtuoso of Chopin and Liszt, whose fingers were like waterfalls that approached the heart of the night. For him, Eva was music. In Prague at dusk, the passers-by would approach her window to listen to her fingers glide across the keyboard like someone hearing the first steps of God in the night. War arrived, with its signs and wagons of mist, and Eva also marched in the distance amid the hollow sounds of terror. Eva did not safeguard the sadness of exiles or feel the rhythms of flight. Instead she hid her broken and bruised hands and missed the piano, which had become the guardian of her memory.

Eva left Prague in the middle of the night and headed for Hamburg. She had music between her fingers, the *Nocturnes* in her breath, and she arrived at the boat, which was like a lighthouse that would guide her to safety and to the challenges of a new life. In the evenings when the reticent, unsteady boat made its threatening movements and variations, the nocturnal, sleepwalking Eva played her imaginary piano next to the moon, before the vast and magnificent outdoors. In the distance, a passenger gazed at her. He didn't speak Czech and she didn't speak German, but they loved each other through the crisp melodies of waves and fragrances.

Eva hummed old piano melodies many nights during the threatening ocean swells, until they arrived at Arica Harbor on the northern tip of Chile. Neither of them knew how to speak Spanish and neither of them had even thought of what it would be like to arrive at the shores of a lost and generous South American continent through the distances that they had travelled. She then whispered in his ear as if what she said had something to do with the arpeggios of memory, and told him that they would meet again beyond the calendars and seasons. This is what she told him in Czech and Mr. Fishman, the German, understood and smiled like a butterfly that survives all the vicissitudes of the harsh outdoors.

These strange foreigners found themselves in the middle of the Arica desert, gathering the orange blossoms of memory, somnolent and dreamy in this transparent and luminous geography. Years later, on one warm afternoon of idleness and thirst, Mr. Fishman decided to go to the movies—and there was Eva, playing the piano with an absentminded gaze during the film intermissions. Perhaps she was imagining the streets of Prague, the grief of the deranged and the perseverance of memory. He recognized her, and through the fragrance of the music that he had kept for so many years, he approached and kissed her after the intermission. Afterwards, they finally returned home together. They crossed the slopes of the dunes, that landscape with the harrowing sun that was so foreign yet now so familiar–distant from Prague and Hamburg, but a place they could love each other between the nocturnes and share a reconciliatory kiss after all the wars and all the rains.

This is the love story that my father told me in at twilight in Athens, Georgia, as he prepared to play one of Chopin's *Nocturnes* and thought about Eva and about the rituals of love and remembrance.

## Nocturnes

My father is a quiet individual, cautious in his demeanor and with measured pauses always filling his speech. However, when he plays the piano it seems as if he becomes slim, weightless and luminous, letting himself be swept up by the heroic tides of the sonatas. When he plays, the piano becomes an even more marvelous and noble instrument, without borders or languages, and my father himself journeys beyond dreams, love, and the stars of the Southern Hemisphere.

My father's first serious illness was caused by a small clot in the brain that occurred precisely when he was playing Chopin. My mother found him sprawled out and apparently lifeless on the floor. For many months he could not approach his friend, the open piano. He felt betrayed by life, as if the grief of the piano had penetrated the layers of his skin. After a year, he returned to music although to date, he still does not play Liszt or Chopin's *Nocturnes*.

I think of my father and imagine him with his hands on the keys, defying death.

# SANTIAGO

## Capital of Dreams and Fugues

### 1940–1968

## Rain in the Southern Hemisphere

The drizzle immobilizes the city. Throughout the dawn, the rain sketches its minute patterns on the sidewalks. The strong seasonal winds blow off the hat of little Moshka, now a seventeen-year-old medical student who left behind the city of churches and violet-haired, perfumed ladies in order to study medicine at the University of Chile, where he could dream about being a first-rate scientist and an accomplished pianist.

On his way to the university, Moshka crosses the cemetery, carrying his mascot, the skeleton that would accompany him during the years of insomnia and solitude. He calls it Luchito, the beloved fragile and smiling cadaver, an angel who smiles between the waxing darkness of night and day and does not fear the avatars of life.

In Santiago, Moshka is viewed with suspicion because of his premature baldness, because of his habit of walking about with a skeleton, and because he is a young Jewish boy who aspires to be a doctor and plays the piano at dawn.

## Santiago, 1941

My father left Quillota, with its avocado pears and immense promenades lined with poplars. He arrived in Santiago in 1941. He says that before leaving, my grandmother kissed her little Moses, saved from the water, in the middle of his prematurely bald head, for he was on his way to being a doctor—the dream of every Jewish mother about to be fulfilled. She then put on her patent leather shoes and her felt, violet-colored hat and sang a beautiful Turkish lullaby.

A diminutive and solitary figure, my father departed for Santiago. His father left him at a boarding house in the most abandoned and somber part of the city. Moisés arrived at Mrs. Guzman's shabby boarding house with a suit and fifty books of music. Here, in one of the oldest neighborhoods of Santiago, sleepless bohemians and cross-eyed poets would gather together. Mrs. Guzman suffered from toothaches and she would wail whenever she remembered them. She also suffered from a religious fervor that resembled mad love passions.

This lady went to mass five or six times a day. Intrigued, my father tried to determine the cause of this religious ardor and to find out if it had something to do with those dreadful toothaches. The mystery of the frequent visits to the altar was soon discovered. This woman, wearing a dark dress, went to church to relieve herself of the enormous sin of having a Jewish boarder— a Jew who paid her every week for the privilege of room and board, but a Jew nonetheless, descended from an evil line of hunchbacks and foreigners.

## Wartime

My father had an education grounded in the humanities. He was an avid reader of books of love and of chivalry, but he wanted to be a scientist and chose to go to medical school, where Jews were once again a minority. In time he would become the only Jewish full professor in the school.

If the isolation and polarization of the high school years in Quillota were marked by the signs and rituals of prejudice, during the period in which my father studied medicine, the hatreds of the war acquired the strength of evil passions.

At that time there were only three Jewish students in a class of approximately one thousand in the medical school at the University of Chile. The professors of medicine, trained at the devoutly Catholic Academy of St. Lucas, were faithful guardians of anti-Semitic traditions. The Catholicism of the time was fervent and, paradoxically, linked to the ideology of the Third Reich. The war produced a strong polarization between the students who favored the Third Reich and those who supported the Allies; the latter were in the minority. There were frequent confrontations between these groups.

My father could not walk through the medical school alone without exposing himself to physical attacks.

As he walked home from the university, the student
would often hit my father and call him a *judio sucio*,
dirty Jew, and one time a German medical student tried
to cut off one of his ears. For many years he would receive
sinister phone calls at dawn threatening him with
death. Not easily dissuaded, he would carry a small cam-
ouflage knife in his pocket and some husky friends would
accompany him and protect him from evil omens
while he walked through the old, dilapidated hall-
ways of the medical school.

## Skeletons

My father loved the study of medicine. He always
loved microscopes and minute things, crystals and
obsidian mirrors, things that were concave, and he
loved the chaos of order. For our birthdays years later
he would give us small insect collections, and when we
turned ten years old, a thimble with invisible threads.

My father always talked respectfully about the dead.
He actually knew how to speak with the dead in a low
and melodious voice. This was due to the fact that as a
student, whenever he would leave the Guzman boarding house and head for the medical school, he would pass
by the public cemetery and turn right at the morgue.
Anatomy lessons were among his favorite classes.
When the gravediggers would see the poor young medical student pass by with his white jacket and immense
bag, they would offer him dead bodies at modest prices.

In the evenings, when Moisés would return to the Guzman boarding house, the landlady would cross herself upon seeing him, while a priest on Maule Street continued blaming Jews for the death of Christ. This was the message I grew up with, and so too my father, and in all likelihood my grandparents when they were in Odessa and Sebastopol. We grew up with the catechism that was recited to us as in an hallucinatory chorus: "Who killed Christ?" "The Jews killed Christ." And sometimes would repeat it and cry singing it.

## The Doctors

At that time, many doctors were among the numbers of Jewish refugees—limited by strict quotas—who came to Chile with slashed suitcases, displacing themselves to avoid the horrors of extermination. They arrived as lost souls in a world where the sharp light of the Southern Hemisphere did not permit hiding places or masks.

My father met many of these doctors, and learned from them while he pursued his vocation. They had been trained at the most important medical centers of Vienna and Hamburg. However, in Santiago, the doctors at the Academy of St. Lucas did not permit them to practice. The new immigrants were forced to travel to abandoned provinces in the middle of the forests and the pampa. No one offered them a helping hand—only exile to remote and miserable provinces, where ignorance and

hatred affected their daily lives, and where the citizen
were dominated by fear. Many of those who traveled
to southern Chile found themselves nearly as persecuted
there as they had been in Berlin or Prague. They were
nevertheless, good samaritans, who cured without
expecting either gratitude or respect; they simply
cured because this was their mission in life.

## Calculus

During his first year in medical school, my father studied calculus with a taciturn and Marxist professor who
lived in an isolated neighborhood in Santiago. His
name was Rubén Azócar. Years later I learned that his
sister Albertina was the first and greatest love of Don
Pablo Neruda, our national poet. My father said that he
would arrive at the home of the master mathematician
hoping to see Albertina, desolate and pale, silent and
distant, contemplating the late afternoon sky and the
appearance of the first stars in the heavens. Albertina,
however, never showed up; only Neruda, always
solemn and wearing his black owl cape.

## Medicine in Chile, I

My father's years as a medical student were terrifying,
sinister, and at the same time beautiful, emphasizing the
complexity of his Judaism. He delighted in the pleasures of being self-taught, of reading everything that fell

into his hands and having sufficient time to meditate over the purifying harmony of the abstract sciences and the pleasures of memory. However, Chilean society in the decade of the forties was dominated by men with distinguished surnames–the landowners with supposedly noble ancestors. The sons of some of these men studied medicine, and would not for anything in the world associate themselves with the vulgar Masons and Jews. The good people belonged to the Academy of St. Lucas. They were devout Catholics who believed that Jews had horns like Michelangelo's Moses and that they bathed in the blood of Christ on days of resurrection. When they became acquainted with my father, some whispered that they hadn't seen his horns.

Throughout the 1940s, Jews were barely allowed to study medicine or even work in clinics. No work was given to the Jewish refugee doctors who had occupied important positions in European clinics. Instead they were humiliated by people who would not show even a hint of compassion toward these tattooed beings, destroyed by the devastation of war.

In those years, a great chasm separated the small minority who possessed land, and therefore wealth, and the majority who did not. The political history of my country has always been characterized by these great divisions of power and land, status and "connections."

One of the goals of the government of Salvador Allende, three decades later, was to attempt to change these deeply rooted structures. However, the oligarchy triumphed, and a fascist ruler assumed power for almost seventeen years. Today, under a democracy, Chile continues to be governed as if it were a small feudal kingdom, run by people with the same surnames and wealth. The same families who held power in the thirties and forties have recovered power and once again govern the country. Their servants wear white gloves and aprons, while sophisticated ladies ring delicate little silver bells and silently cover their overstuffed mouths while eating. In feudal meetings, even today, individuals assure themselves of a great Jewish plot to overthrow the government. They laugh and strangely become speechless when my grandmother slips off her glove and reveals the tattoo of memory.

## Friends

My father had few friends during the years that he studied to become one of the few Jewish doctors in Chile. But he remembers with great fondness certain study companions. René Christen was—and continued to be until his recent death—one of my father's best friends, in spite of the fact that he was of German ancestry and had relatives who were fascists. René himself always revealed through his generous actions the inclinations of a true democrat.

René had a great obsession with shoes and liked to show them off, taking advantage of the opportunity to criticize my father, who never kept up with the styles and often wore shoes that needed a shine. Moisés would tell René that he couldn't bend over to clean his shoes because of a physical handicap, and the two of them would continue walking through the city squares. They would sit on park benches to eat roasted peanuts, as they thought about music and life, which at that time was modest and busy.

During his early years in medical school, René and other friends lived in a boarding house of the Catholic university, which was strictly prohibited to Jews. My father, therefore, wandered from boarding house to boarding house, taking cold showers and eating tasteless food.

## Enemies

Among his classmates at medical school, my father also remembers Hans, who still lives and practices medicine in the ominous pro-Nazi towns in southern Chile. According to my father, Hans was a shy and delicate youth who played the violin well from a technical point of view, but whose passion and affection were feigned while he played. Hans was an extremely rich young man. His parents owned one of the most prestigious optical shops in Chile, but Hans kept this secret, as if all of the facts that others could discover about his life were dangerous. He kept too many secrets, and among the things he tried to hide was his anti-Semitism.

Since my father loved music, they would often talk

about arpeggios and sonatas, but Hans in moments of strange and perverted humor would say: "Moisés, it is impossible to maintain a conversation with most Jews because they are so vulgar and loud. But you are different." Without responding, my father would reach for his weighty chemistry books with the colorful illustrations and would take off for the boarding house where he lived and where the landlady prayed and asked God for forgiveness for having given lodging to a Jew.

In anatomy class, Hans discovered that someone had written the word *Jew* in his notebook in immense red letters. When he shouted out in a desperate rage, my father simply asked him why the word *Jew* was so offensive to him. Hans conducted a grand investigation to find the guilty party. His family called lawyers, and in the end they accused my father because he was the only Jew in the class. Among the fifty students in the class, they thought that only someone like Moisés Agosín could have written the word *Jew* in red letters.

When my father tells this story he wonders why it was considered a crime to write the word *Jew* in a notebook, but it was not a criminal offense to tattoo the arms of women and children as if they were helpless animals in the hidden zones of the war waged by civilized Germany.

## Doña Josefina's Boarding House

My father's memories of this time at the university are not kind ones. The exception is the years when he lived at the home of my maternal grandmother, Josephine, who was the daughter of Marcos Agosín, the millionaire tailor and my grandfather Abraham's brother. Josephine's daughter Frida, still a high school student, was extraordinarily beautiful, with violet-colored eyes. My mother fell in love with Moisés while he cared for my ailing great-grandmother Helena.

Since there was no great difference in age between Moisés and Frida, with time they realized that they had common interests, that they found each other mutually pleasant, and that perhaps they could begin a relationship with a future. Thus, before my father finished his medical studies, he and my mother became engaged. This, according to my father, was the best decision of his life.

## Ancestry

When my maternal grandparents came to South America, to the zones of glaciers and blizzards, they brought their clothing and a gentility in their walk. They didn't discard their language, but simply lived as Europeans in a country they called the land of the barbarians. My mother, like many of her generation, learned German from her grandmother, Helena. This occurred more among the German and Viennese Jews, who had lived a secular rather than a Jewish orthodox life.

Among my father's relatives, most of whom were tailors, Russian was never spoken; even at home, Odessa and Sebastopol were sealed off in the annals of memory. Nevertheless, a conspiratorial alliance has always existed between parents and children and grandparents, connected by time and the sorrows of exile—loving relatives returning to an apprenticeship of love.

## Dr. Agosín

When my father received his degree in medicine in 1948, his conscience forced him to debate numerous ethical and moral problems. He pondered, for instance, how to charge the sick, those haggard beings who were dispossessed by fate and by the poverty of their birth. Sometimes those who were incapable of paying him with money gave him eggs and fresh figs, and the most indigent among them gave him pieces of semi-fresh meat.

Visiting hospitals in Santiago was like entering abandoned houses, with their smells of rancid and maimed solitude. There my father encountered faces full of fear and the vulnerable bodies of prostrated and submissive patients. All the indifference, poverty, and chaos of Latin America was exposed in those hospitals, in those faces that implored relentlessly for a little tea with lemon for curing spasms. My father, so short in his white coat, resembling a ghost or a sweet wizard, learned to console his patients by taking their hands and restoring their usurped dignity. He also realized, however, that he could not heal poverty and that his conscience would not allow him to charge the sick, who were far more miserable than he.

Practicing medicine was for my father a confusing, difficult, and morally precarious profession. For this reason he chose to continue with his research projects and his studies in parasitology. All these contradictory feelings led him to apply for a Rockefeller Foundation grant in Washington, D.C. In 1950, my father left Chile for the first time and headed north with my young and beautiful mother, who had never cut her copper colored braids so that they could save the money she might have spent on hairdressers.

Thus, with his elf-like doctor's bag, he headed toward other territories. He decided to gaze with wonder at the smallest, most magical creatures of the earth. He dedicated his life to studying insects and the passionate lives of flies, but he always remembered those faces in the hospital in Santiago.

## Washington and the Cold War

The foundations of my parents' Yankee experience were laid in Washington, D.C., the city of squirrels, sunflowers, and earth colored parks. My parents rented a dark basement apartment in Bethesda, Maryland. They would wander through the gardens of the city, the museums and the old neighborhoods, on luminous days warmed by that exquisite, tender, and tepid sun so loved by the lizards. Washington was at that time a city without violence, like almost all the cities in the United States where people would leave the doors to their homes and cars unlocked. However, there was a latent danger hidden in a racism whose origins could be traced to the arrival of slaves on American soil.

My father says that sometimes he and my mother were looked at with suspicion because of their strange accents, but since they were both fair-skinned and my mother had violet-colored eyes, they weren't questioned much and were allowed to enter restaurants that were open to whites only.

During that time, my father recalls, it was not unusual to see men on the streets of the capital with missing limbs and faces anguished by pain and sadness. There were also men in wheelchairs pushed by catatonic wives. This was one legacy of the Cold War: the remains of shattered human beings, the phantom victims of the Korean War. Very little was said about that war, as is the case in many conflicts that nations fight in distant zones with apparent disinterest, with a passion for justice that in the end becomes a passion for control and wealth.

In Washington my parents lived the experience of the Cold War, when McCarthyism was at its height. They were idealists, raised in the "Third World," with socialist tendencies, and they were troubled by the secret terror that swarmed in the dense and sinister air.

At the National Institutes of Health there was a young biochemist who had a good sense of humor and was great at square dancing, his only vice and passion. Suddenly, one day, he disappeared from the offices of the NIH, and no one ever saw him again or even bothered to ask what had happened to him. His removal resembled the many disappearances of people that would take place years later in Chile and Argentina. After a short while, my father discovered that the young man had been arrested and fired from his job for the sole crime of possessing a Russian surname and being the son of Russian immigrants who were naturalized American citizens. This was all that was needed to consider a good man and worthy scientist a danger to national security. The government officials said that since the matter involved a government-funded laboratory, the administrators could not permit the presence of probable spies and communists on its grounds.

My father always spoke with mistrust about Senator McCarthy. Years later, when Pinochet was in power in Chile, my father used to say that this senator contributed more than any other politician to inciting hatred, mistrust, and violence against communist countries. His activities in the 1950s paved the way for the United States' secret war against the socialist Salvador Allende in the 1970s, and its support for the dictatorship of Pinochet, which exiled my father permanently from his country.

## Embassy Parties

When my parents lived in Washington, they had diplomatic passports because of the grants that my father had been awarded. As a result, they were always invited to the parties at the Chilean embassy. Although they were withdrawn and timid, they accepted the invitations with pleasure and a sense of solidarity, so that they would feel less lonely and be able to speak Spanish, enjoying themselves in their own language. My father often talks about how the military "attaches" arrogantly advertised their wealth by telling everyone, in their half-intoxicated state, that they earned three times more than the President of the United States. Other frequent guests at these receptions told my father that Chile was striving to preserve the purity of the blood of its inhabitants—by which they meant European Christian blood—although they themselves showed clear signs of indigenous heritage. My father simply smiled and remained silent. How strange for a descendant of the assassinated Mapuche villager to be worried about preserving purity of the blood. As I recall these subtle and disorderly images, I think of a desperate and servile Chile, overflowing with racial hostility.

## City of My Birth

During my parents' first visit to Washington, D.C., and the "real" America, my sister Cynthia and then I myself were born in a small hospital in Bethesda, Maryland. My mother says that I was very tiny and bald and that I lived for months in an incubator. Perhaps it was there that my love of secrets and vaulted chambers and my childhood passion for hiding in closets were born. It was in our small apartment outside the United States capital that my sister and I first learned to walk and to curtsy. Although we soon returned to Chile, the happenstance of our birthplace became part of our long-term destiny: we were both United States citizens.

## The Beauty of Objects

One of the most fruitful periods of my father's life was his time in Washington, D.C. Fine and modest scientists like the Nobel laureate in medicine Andre Lwoff came to that laboratory. At the National Institutes of Health, my father made deep and glorious friendships with individuals who continue to visit us today. In Bethesda, my father accomplished some of his greatest scientific achievements, working with Theodor Von Brand in the area of tropical medicine. Professor Von Brand was generous and benevolent. He taught my father that it was not enough to look at objects with love;

it was necessary to also look at them carefully so as no
to miss their beauty.

## Grace

We returned to Chile on the ocean liner *Grace,* which
carried both cargo and passengers. Priests and nuns were
among the voyagers. We were the only nonbelievers
on board; what we prayed for was a good education
We arrived at the same harbor in Valparaíso that had
greeted both my Viennese maternal grandparents and
my paternal grandparents on their journey from
Marseilles. Viewed from the water, Valparaíso always
seems restless and preciously confused. People carry
bags of bread and honey and seem like flowers descending from the hills. The city has a fragrance associated
with early times, with men and women strolling in the
stillness of the night, exchanging stories of sea voyages
and of young brides running down the hills, barefoot
and in love.

## Mariners

When I came to Chile I arrived by sea, repeating the
exploits and voyages of my great-grandparents, my grandparents, my uncles, and my father. This is why I have
always been a mariner—a lover of water, of rocks,
and of that which exists in the wavy depths. They say
that I was very beautiful and tiny then, and that when

my mother disembarked on the Chilean shore with me in September 1955, a porter said, "Señora, may I carry the doll?"

## Professor of Medicine

Nineteen sixty-two was a pivotal year in my father's academic life in Chile. His former teacher, the distinguished parasitologist Amador Neghme, invited him to apply for the position of director and chair of medical chemistry at the University of Chile in Santiago, since the department at the university was highly deficient in scientific training and practice. Old professors obliged their students to memorize very long names of medicines together with their esoteric prescriptions that had a closer resemblance to alchemy than to the exact sciences.

My father presented his candidacy and for a long time during the deliberations he received anonymous threats, calls at three or four in the morning, all anti-Semitic, asking him to renounce his candidacy or else they would kill him and his wife and his two daughters. Dead cats were left on our doorsteps, and as my sister and I left school, threatening phone calls would come in, proving that we were being watched.

My brave and obstinate father continued with his candidacy in spite of the fact that a group of old professors at the university met with the medical dean, Don Jorge Alessandri, and told him that a matter of conscience prevented them from voting. In other words, they couldn't vote for a Jew. Nevertheless, in December 1962 my father was selected as the chair of the Department of Medical Chemistry, becoming the first Jewish professor elected to that position since the founding of the university in 1842. To this day, there have been no others.

In March 1963, when classes commenced for the new academic year, the assistants in medical chemistry resigned collectively because they didn't want to work with a Jew. As a result, my father was unable to give his lab classes. Gradually he hired new personnel and invigorated a dying department. Under my father's leadership, an extraordinary number of high-quality professional papers emanating from the department were published throughout the world. This was among his most important legacies, together with the gratitude of his committed students and their ethical responsibility in matters having to do with science and the betterment of humanity.

It was difficult for all of us, including me at such a tender age, to accept the fact that many of my father's friends, who visited our house and stayed drinking wine until very late at night, had refused to vote for him and had resigned because their conscience would not allow them to believe in a Jew.

## The Luminous Years

In the early sixties, my father, together with other less corrupt souls who had forgotten their prejudices, worked in one of the most dynamic research labs in Latin America. Energetic scientists published their first papers and, as was customary, there were numerous criticisms from a biased foreign scientific community that did not want to acknowledge the accuracy and precision of scientists from the "Third World."

Among the outstanding visitors who came to our country and also to our house, I remember the Israeli-U.S. toxicologist, Albert Perry, our longtime friend, who later received us with open arms during our exile in the United States. I also recall the Nobel Prize laureate Linus Pauling and Doctor Theodor Von Brand, who had become one of my father's dearest friends. Doctor Von Brand spoke not only English, French and German, but also perfect Spanish.

During one of our summer reunions, when the conversation and red wine flowed with happiness, Von Brand told us that he belonged to the German aristocracy and held the title of Baron. Nevertheless, his family left Germany in fear in 1932 and headed for Scandinavia, eventually reaching the United States. Even noble titles could not protect a Jew in Nazi Germany, and the doctor was the grandson of the great industrialist and Jewish philanthropist Baron von Hirsch, who had helped many Jews migrate to Argentina in the 1800s.

## Medicine in Chile, II

Medicine in Chile, since its beginnings, was dominated by those who belonged to the rancid aristocracy, owners of great country estates and people with fancy last names who treated the Jews and mestizos like feudal subjects and the indigenous people like slaves. I myself remember that during the years when my father held the much coveted chair in chemistry at the medical school, colleagues would call him asking him why he wasn't living in his own country. My father would respond by asking them which country they were referring to. Was it France and the disheveled port of Marseilles? "No," they answered, "Israel." Their unspoken message was: "Get out of our country, you Jew!"

There were certain positions at the university that Jews were specifically prevented from holding–gynecology, among them. Many of my father's friends had to leave the capital and practice in the provinces because it was impossible for them to have a professional and personal life in the city. My father would become speechless whenever he would hear statements like: "You should be practicing medicine among your own kind."

## The Development of Science

What always caught our attention in Chile's small towns were the many churches constantly under repair. These repairs lasted years without any visible signs of progress. We could never figure out the reasons for these delays. They might have been due to poor construction schemes, to the slowness of the workers, or to difficulties with the acquisition of materials. However, the possibility that the delays were also a means of getting donations over the years could not be entirely ruled out.

My father told me about a case involving plans for the medical school at the University of Chile, which had been lost in a fire in 1947. Certain buildings still have not been reconstructed. It seems as if the whole country is and always will be under repair, with its history and characters suspended in a permanent construction project.

This phenomenon, according to my father, occurs in the financing of the infrastructure in the sciences in Chile as well. When we lived in Bethesda in the fifties, we received a phone call from the man who was then dean of the medical school, and was visiting in Washington. He wanted to speak with my father at nine o'clock the following morning, apparently on a matter of great urgency. Having no other choice, my father appeared punctually at nine at the hotel where the dean was staying. Soon after he arrived, the dean appeared carrying a huge quantity of architectural plans for the new medical school. This happened in 1953.

Of course, the medical school, which is enormous, still remains unfinished in 1996. This is due to economic difficulties but also to the ineptitude of the construction companies in charge of this monumental project. The heating system turned out to be so inefficient that it only worked on the day that it was installed. Fuel expenses were so high that they consumed almost the entire budget, and the elevators that were installed with great fanfare, including the service elevators, turned out to be limited to a capacity of two people each. As a result, heavy equipment needed to be transported to the higher floors by means of the stairs. Accidents occurred during these moves, and many times equipment was destroyed and people were injured.

The inefficiency also spread to the administration. Since the bulk of the equipment and supplies required by the researchers came from abroad, several companies had representatives in Chile to whom university administrators would send their purchase orders. But all this was done without obtaining competitive quotes, so that the university always ended up paying the highest prices.

In addition, the same dean who years earlier had proudly shown my father the plans for the medical school received a considerable grant in U.S. currency from the Rockefeller Foundation for the purchase of intercoms for the new buildings. The dean exchanged the U.S. dollars for Chilean currency and deposited the sum in a local bank. Twenty-four hours later the Chilean peso was devalued fifty percent. When the Rockefeller Foundation discovered the poor management of its funds, it withdrew its support. Needless to say the intercoms were never installed.

The realities of life in Chile meant that Chilean science lost more than funding. Some great scientists who still had much to contribute to the academy, like Herman Niemeyer and Osvaldo Cori, died prematurely. But even more tragically, an entire generation of researchers were lost either through emigration or because they were forced to leave the universities or change careers because of pressures from the government.

## Occupations

Chile is such a strange and beautiful country, eccentric and oblivious, where poets are diplomats and presidential candidates and where precision and mathematics are confused. Economists are playwrights, clowns govern, and I can only guess at what architects do.

## The Future of Medicine

One of my father's constant concerns, as much on a professional as on a personal and ethical level, has been to develop genuine, well-prepared scientists in Chile. For many years, my father and other scientists tried to convince the council at the University of Chile to create a school of advanced scientific studies, charged with providing in-depth training to biologists, biochemists, physicists, and mathematicians.

But Chile has long been a country fearful of change. It took years for this science school to be approved. In

1964 this unique center at the university was located on Maule Street next to my school, the Hebrew Institute. When we were pupils, we would fall in love watching those long-haired students making mathematical signs on the pavement.

My father was invited to the University of London in 1965. Upon his return he discovered that all of his colleagues who had participated in the development of the School of Sciences had been appointed as professors of the new faculty, but he had not. This, for him, was Chilean gratitude.

## England

In early 1965 my father received an invitation from the University of London to participate in a program having to do with resistance to insecticides. He was not very excited about it because all research performed there was purely biological. What the English scientists wanted was a more modern focus, and this is why they solicited my father's assistance. By this time the third Agosín child had arrived, and my parents were reluctant to leave my newborn brother Mario behind with family. Yet my father wanted to take advantage of the visit so that he could later go to Jerusalem and continue the discussion he had begun about a position at Hebrew University. In any event, my parents eventually left for England and I was delighted to know that they would be visiting the land of the Beatles.

The room that was reserved for them at the hotel was too small, so they spent a while searching for an apartment that wasn't far from the university. They finally got a flat in Bayswater, which made it necessary for them to use the underground in order to go to the university. This was not a very pleasant experience during rush hour, but it was better than the enchanting but slow two-tiered buses.

The reality of the famous British work ethic, which had won wars and built empires, was less challenging than the myth. No one ever arrived before nine o'clock in the morning. At approximately ten o'clock they drank tea and ate cookies in a small library. At twelve noon they ate in the university cafeteria; at three o'clock they served tea again; and at four o'clock people began to leave the university to avoid the horrendous rush-hour traffic. The infrastructure was, likewise, a revelation to a "Third World" scientist. In fact, the laboratories were small and poorly equipped, while the offices were roomy and well-furnished. This configuration seems to be common in all of Europe, since my father had seen it in Italy, Sweden, and Finland, as well as in Israel. But it was contrary to all that my father had experienced in the United States, where the offices were intolerably small and the laboratories spacious and well-lighted.

In accordance with the reserved temperament of the English, my father did not exactly receive a warm reception from his colleagues. This allowed him to dedicate all of his time to working with a graduate student, a young South African who was finishing his doctorate. They compared the level of resistance to insecticides on various types of insects and got important results. These results were submitted for publication to a Dutch journal. However, as had happened previously, it took a while for them to be published. When they finally were published, they appeared along with papers by Dutch scientists refuting the results of my father's research. Since my father and his colleagues considered the results of their study irrefutable, they chose to ignore this unfortunate incident.

London fascinated my parents, especially its love of tradition, its magnificent museums, and the great artistic activity in the city. They visited the countryside thanks to the kindness of the South African student, but their best moments were spent with Daniel Labworth and his wife. Daniel's mother, who was from the Ukraine, was the aunt of my mother's maternal grandmother. Through a series of circumstances she had ended up in England, where she began a small business selling cardboard boxes. With time this business became a large factory, which eventually was managed by Daniel. All of the cigarette packaging that was produced in England was manufactured at this plant. Through Daniel my parents were invited to the Bar Mitzvah of the son of his friends. The invitation was extremely formal and my parents were asked how they wished to be announced—as Doctor Agosín, Mr. Agosín, or Professor Agosín and wife. They chose Professor to counteract their lack of formal clothing. Upon arriving at the party site my mother and father were astonished by the number of automobiles parked in front of the premises—most of them Rolls Royces, including some antiques, and a few Jaguars. My mother also worried about leaving her overcoat in the checkroom until she saw more than two hundred fur coats hanging from the racks. My parents entered the ballroom where a squire with an enormous baton struck the floor three times and announced them. They still remember this event as their most glamorous.

## A Practitioner's Art

Laboratory work for Moisés Agosín constituted the most primordial of his scientific tasks. Many times I saw him pursue flies from strange latitudes and caress vinchuca bugs. My father did all of this with love and humility. During the forties he worked in solitude in small, dark rooms at an impoverished university, where the chill of the winter and the rain made cracks in the floor. He always talked about the "great" professors who would not dirty themselves with lab work and who let the young students do everything, including writing the names of their teachers on their scientific publications.

Recently, my father has told me that the deaths of his friends and loved ones have made him reflect calmly on the large and small injustices that have affected his generation of scientists in Chile and Latin America. Most of all, my father contemplates the lack of acknowledgment for his accomplishments in life and the scorn that he and others received from foreign scientists for their stigmatized "Third World" discoveries.

It is difficult to recreate for the reader the arduous path traveled by Latin American scientists from the 1920s until today. Despite meager resources, they have made extraordinary advances, but they have received little recognition. Even Carlos Finlay, the Cuban scientist who explained how yellow fever is transmitted through insects, received insufficient credit for his remarkable discovery.

The poor recognition of Latin American scientists, especially women, became even clearer to my father in the 1970s, when we emigrated to the United States and he himself became a "Third World" scientist in the eyes of his colleagues. Most of the prizes at that time were awarded to European researchers, and the Europeans, like the Americans, discriminated against the more downtrodden nationalities among them. My father and his colleagues could tell many stories of injustices that were known to all, but difficult to redress: an Italian scientist whose important discovery in parasitology, accomplished in a dilapidated laboratory, was superseded by an inferior study by an Englishman; a Columbian researcher whose introduction of an important new vaccine was dismissed by competitors from the developed world. These are the ways in which the unequal power of nations filters into the esoteric and "pure" world of scientific research.

## Israel

Achieving intellectual stature and economic affluence did not guarantee my family acceptance in the cultural milieu Chile. We did not fit in with the Europeans, who took pride in their supposedly pure bloodlines and their relative "whiteness." But we also did not exactly fit in with the mestizos, or with the indigenous inhabitants, the cholos, who were spat upon in the streets. As Jews we were looked upon with suspicion or sometimes pity. We were Europeans, but our heritage belonged to no European nation. Our position was both strange and ambivalent. We understood that Chile was a transient land in our existence as wanderers in borrowed territories. Israel presented us with a possible alternative.

Although my father's Judaism was defined more by his life experiences than by his religious beliefs, Israel occupied an almost magical and mystical place in his conversations with us. For my father Israel was not a haven for persecuted Jews, nor was it the only possible place of return from perpetual exile. Israel, instead, represented the possibility of a new form of life, a life in which identity could be felt as something visceral. My father did not worry so much about belonging to a community, but rather belonging to the earth, to a beloved landscape, a type of lost ancestral paradise. Since he had never been in Israel, however, my father was not sure it would be a place where he could feel at home.

I remember that Santiago awakened snow-covered on the first day of the Six-Day War in 1967. Astounded by the whiteness and filled with illusions, we gazed through the window of dreams that fogged up with our breath as my father announced that war had broken out in Israel. The phone calls began soon after, and Christian friends told us how sorry they felt for our loss. My school, the prestigious Hebrew Institute, closed its doors and flew the flag at half mast. But, six days later, when the war ended, we felt free. Israel was safe; it was still there if we needed it,

For a long time at home we talked about a possible trip to Israel, and on various occasions my father received invitations to visit. In 1966 the possibility of emigrating became a reality. My father had received an offer to become the chairman of the parasitology department at Hebrew University. Our move, he said, would not be a religious pilgrimage, but rather a recognition of the social, political, and educational values of the state of Israel. My father was always proud of belonging to a people with so much historical and moral transcendence. And meanwhile, in Chile, the ignorant continued calling him a "dirty Jew" and telling him to return to "his country."

The day after the offer came through, my mother organized the first "garage sale" in the history of Chile. We moved the huge dining room table to the garden next to the doves, lizards, and chickens of our loyal Carmencita, my mother's beloved nanny and confidant. All the while my mother felt happy and in charge. However, we never went to Israel. My father decided not to accept the position.

A year later, my father was received by the dean of medicine at Hebrew University together with other important colleagues, among them Professor Saul Adler, one of the few extraordinary members of the Royal Society of England. Adler was looking for someone of international stature who would be worthy to replace him because he was dying of cancer. My father had no doubt that the department needed to be renovated. The majority of the professors were advanced in years, the direction of the research was fundamentally biological, the offices and labs were austere, and the equipment was outdated. In his response, my father said that if they gave him the opportunity to hire young people and provided adequate space for laboratories, he would consider the offer. They also discussed the problem of salaries, which were relatively low, but which my father hoped to complement with foreign scholarships and other sources of funding. The dean promised to have a laboratory equipped for my father within a year, and he returned to Chile.

In 1967, right after a trip to Geneva, my father returned once again to Israel, where he encountered many disappointments. First, he discovered that the chairmanship had been offered to him in a very irregular manner. The faculty therefore convened and voted for my father again. It appears that this action was necessary because another member of the department desired the position. Other troubling news had to do with the laboratories. Even though more than a year had transpired since my father's earlier visit, nothing had been done because the individual in charge of expanding and modernizing the labs had accepted an appointment at another university. Taking all this into account, in addition to the low salary, my father thought it prudent to suspend his conversations with the Israeli university, not knowing that in the near future he would regret his decision. Soon we would instead undertake a long and bewildering exile in the United States, where we would be perceived not as Jews but as Latin Americans—but still as foreigners and inferiors.

## Santiago, 1967

It is snowing in the city. For the first time in twenty years, the children of the shanty towns of an invisible Santiago, surrounded by barricades, hunger, and truncated lives, walk toward the high-rent district amid the hallucinatory whiteness. They make enormous snowmen, whose heads they adorn with red carnations. We, the children of the high-rent district, have lost our sense of wonder before the whiteness. We are the sons and daughters of doctors and skiers whose children go to private schools. Nevertheless, there is something within me that draws me to the children of the shanty town. I approach them and we throw snowballs at each other. Minutes later I see my father arrive, crestfallen and taciturn. One of his ears is wounded and little drops of blood embellish the whiteness of the landscape. Someone called him a "dirty Jew" and threw a rock at him, grazing his ear. I will always remember that first snowfall of the season— the air that was so transparent, and my father's ear, dripping delicate drops, leaving behind impressions, red petals on the whiteness and the shadows.

## Nineteen Sixty-Eight

In the year 1968, there was an insurgence of political activity in the student community worldwide. It was the year of revolts at the Sorbonne, and also at the University of Chile. Students demanded the right to participate in the hiring of professors and in the selection of courses. At that time my father occupied the chair in chemistry at the medical school at the University of Chile. Because of his prominence in research, he was supported by grants from the Ford and Rockefeller Foundations as well as the NIH. In spite of the fact that my father was and continues to be a liberal, noble in his principles of justice, ethics, and leadership, he was nevertheless accused of selling out to Yankee imperialism because he worked with money from the United States. Few knew that he was a Jewish liberal. However, neither the Communists nor the Christian

Democrats wanted him, neither the left nor the right, and they began to make his life impossible, locking the door to his laboratory and letting his animals die. They also threatened him with death. His name appeared in all the newspapers of the city of Santiago, along with the names of his family members. He would return home each day in a broken state, distinguished by the terrible grief of being misunderstood. This is why we had to leave the country, forced by the avatars of a history foreign to his ideology.

I recall the day when my father shut down his laboratory in Santiago forever. This was the lab where the most advanced biochemical research in Chile had taken place. There, among the most arid deserts and most hollow blizzards, the new values of Chilean science were being formed.

The young students who knew in their hearts that Dr. Agosín was not, as the national press had said, a collaborator of Yankee imperialism, sorrowfully witnessed the closing of this great laboratory.

## A Divided Nation

My parents, though not socialists, supported the candidacy of Salvador Allende in 1970. Voting in Chile was a popular yet formal event. It seemed as if people were going to a party dressed in their Sunday best. Allende's triumph made many in the populace euphoric and filled others with enormous anguish and despair. Several Jewish friends left the country, as many of their relatives would later on during the military dictatorship. Those citizens who feared a communism of blacklists and terror left behind their homes, complete with bridal trousseaus and memories of fate and love, carrying their keys with them for their possible return.

However, the real and frightening enemy was not Dr. Salvador Allende with the green gaze and goblin hands. The true enemy appeared two years later. He was the dictator Augusto Pinochet Ugarte, who persecuted all "subversives"—even those who dressed differently, like hairdressers from working-class neighborhoods. Chile became a nation divided among the shadows, besieged by opaque zones of hatred, prejudice, and the ignorance of fear.

My father anticipated all this; he knew that there would be no place, amid the battles of left and right, for a lover of laboratories and of Bach, for an independent thinker, for a Jew.

## The Resilience of Hatred

In the early 1960s, Jean Paul Sartre had made several profound statements claiming that anti-Semitism was something that went beyond the Jewish question in the sense that it represented an attitude toward life. In Chile, anti-Semitism remained resilient through periods of cultural change and political upheaval; it endured.

In the early stages of the Popular Unity Party, and

with the rise of Salvador Allende, a large number of the leaders appointed by the new government, especially the chiefs of staff in the hospitals, were Jews. With very little discretion and a great deal of bad taste, certain factions of the press accused the Jews of taking over the new government and the Popular Unity Party. A few years later, when the Allende government fell and Pinochet rose to power, these same Jewish leaders crossed the Andean cordillera on mules, while others disguised themselves as nuns and priests. We were already living in the United States and we welcomed them, giving them a place to stay, blankets, and love. They were the same friends who had advised my father to join the Communist Party if he didn't want to lose his laboratory. My father preferred to keep his political autonomy instead and he chose exile—or, I should say, exile chose him.

During the Pinochet years medicine was constantly controlled by the fascist forces. It was a known fact that doctors collaborated with the regime, methodically assisting in torture sessions. We also learned of other doctors who refused to participate as accomplices in this cruelty and who were subsequently tortured themselves. As in Argentina, anti-Semitism in Chile left behind its cruelty like a mad omen. Jews were doubly tortured before a sadistic and complicit public like the one that witnessed the *autos-da-fé* during the time of the Inquisition. In Chile, Jews were tortured next to portraits of Hitler.

# Quisco

My family often stayed in a house on the shore, set back from the sea, outlined among the red and dark green pines and humbled by the immense eucalyptus trees. This is where I spent a large part of my childhood. It is also where I got to know my parents, to share their long walks along the rocky paths and to listen as they greeted friends along the way, always prepared to accept invitations to share an afternoon around the fireplace with aromatic wines. My childhood was upholstered by the peace of words, an exchange of aromas, and the noble tastes of friendship. I remember my parents' beloved friend, M. Brodsky, who talked to me about the Berlin Wall and Ché Guevara. At that time I was only eight years old, and I was fascinated by the legends of bearded guerrilla fighters who helped the poor and the Indians. Perhaps I wanted to be like them, which is why I decided to teach the maids of my father's friends as well as the ones in our own home how to read.

As the years passed and the furious times of repression appeared, the homes of my father's friends remained closed. No one greeted us anymore. Quisco became a ghost town populated by drunks, emaciated dogs, and a soldier here and there. Many of our friends crossed the cordillera disguised as monks, others went to the Caribbean, and the most unfortunate perished in houses of torture.

Now I pass by Quisco and remember the bonfires on

the beach, my sister's dances at the town yacht club, and Doña Blanquita's fresh bread. I don't invoke these regions with nostalgia, but only wonder about my father's friends and where they are. Who might have helped them while they were being tortured? With what God might they have pleaded?

## Exiles

We left Chile in 1968, during the height of Salvador Allende's fame. It was then that my father, together with other scientists and intellectuals, undertook what for us would be a wrenching and perpetual exile. We realized that our bodies were destined to cross the Andean range once again, to fulfill dangerous expeditions, to learn other languages and repeat the familiar saga of homeless Jews without a country.

Through the experience of settling in the southern United States, my father managed to understand even more the nomadic history of his ancestors. He told me how he remembered his father, Abraham, and his mother, Raquel, existing as marginal, uninhabited beings through all those years in exile, leaving Russia behind because of political and religious persecution and living in the back room of a shop in Marseilles. He managed to feel, through his own immigrant experience, the heroic efforts of his parents, who had overcome the terrible torment of those without a country, the humiliation suffered by those who speak with an accent, those who must abandon their language, their songs, and their samovars.

When we reached Georgia, in spite of not having taken refuge in intermittent camps, we felt like displaced beings, without a home, a nation, or a language. We felt more and more part of that incredible human tangle of emigrant Jews, without a roof over their heads and filled with oblivion. That is how we came to the United States, abandoning what we loved, repeating the ritual of my grandparents, who carried a handful of earth in their pockets and the keys of their burned homes.

Salvador Allende, who was my maternal grandmother's suitor in his youth, was elected to power in 1970 and was assassinated in 1973. We decided not to return to Chile, not to be part of the illegitimate and fascist government that replaced him. To this day, we live in the United States like strangers, without being from anywhere. We miss certain things, like the long walks along the Pacific coast, where we learned the names of certain flowers and recognized the paths of the lizards and seagulls. We also dream about returning to a small stone house with poppies growing and fresh clothes hanging on the line.

Like our grandparents, we have survived in foreignness. We are dancers, wanderers. When we encounter closed doors, there is always someone waiting for us behind an open window.

# Benevolent and Blossoming Homeland

We left Chile in the warm month of September, the florid month of yellow and violet hues. I trembled looking at my parents' astonished faces, both terrified and silent. We contemplated the Andean range, majestic and elongated as it was in my dreams. I knew that we were leaving behind our language and the trees and that we would no longer play in the same tide pools or count the stars with the same peace and gratitude that one knows and feels in one's own land. No one would tell me secrets in Spanish. From the plane's window we saw my maternal grandfather with his green Viennese cloak and a cigarette in his mouth, making a series of smoke rings for us as he walked hastily and desperately in a circle. He also must have been thinking of the time that he left Vienna as in one nocturnal breath. Before departing, I traced the airplane window, blowing a kiss to my grandfather, to my country, and to the memory of everything that would never be ours in exile.

# Cemeteries of Smoke

My father returns to Santiago and is seized by the memories of the already departed. During his silent strolls along the closed cemeteries of smoke, he approaches the throbbing roots of the city, besieged by itinerant beggars and merchants. It is summer; the passers-by detect his gringo sneakers and his checkered shirt. He no longer walks about downcast like other Chileans. He is a being whose body language, like his clothing, identifies him as a foreigner. As a result, the thieves recognize his vulnerability and they rob him "Chilean style." First he is covered with parsley, the herb of the poor, the most exquisite condiment of all the well-known dishes of popular Chilean cooking. Suddenly two young people approach him carefully to brush it off, and while doing so affably rob him of his wallet with the Visa gold card and some money.

My father doesn't get angry. He understands that it was a twist of fate or some strange way of making justice. Later he informs the police and the maids pray to San Benito, who recovers lost objects. The next day someone comes to the house. It is a policeman in a green uniform who returns the wallet, with the Visa card but without the money. He says that the thief was very considerate when he realized that my father was a foreigner.

Nearby, I listen silently to my parents' voices. They have returned to Chile to converse with legendary time, in order perhaps to reconcile themselves with memory. But how can one reconcile a childhood beneath the mist, without toys and bread crumbs for the return trip home? When I talk with them, they seem to have grown young and lighthearted, as if the memories had focused themselves on those years in which they lived on the farthest corner of the planet, happily and with few pretensions. On Sundays when they strolled through the plazas, they would buy balloons and visit familiar and beloved people, like the organ grinder and the gypsy who would read their palms, as we three children followed along in our joyfulness.

As I talk to them it seems as if they had never left Chile, as if the years in exile in North America were imaginary, borrowed and foreign.

*My mother and me in Santiago, 1955.*

*My great-grandmother Sonia, my mother, and my grandmother Josephine with me and my sister Cynthia in the early 1960s.*

*Myself and my sister on a Sunday at the park in Santiago.*

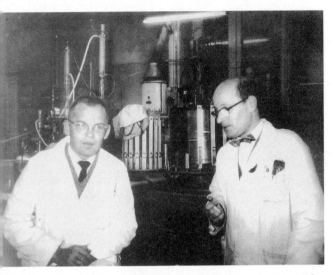

*My father and one of his colleagues at the Department of Biochemistry at the University of California, Berkeley, 1961.*

*My father and me at our summer home in Quisco, 1963.*

*My father at the first Latin American parasitology conference, Santiago, 1967.*

*My parents, my little brother Mario, and me at Quisco in the early 1970s.*

# THE UNITED STATES

*Exiles in a Promised Land*

1968–1997

## The Deep Breath of Exile

All exiles are like deep breaths, imperceptible in uninhabited landscapes. We abandoned our country at night. No one saw us take off. Like fugitives we gazed one more time at the Andean cordillera as the wind created ridges and scars in the dampness of our tear-drenched faces.

## The Melody of Exile

My father always told me that he was always from somewhere else and that he looked at maps to invent cities. He also said that his parents had told him that he was always from somewhere else and that he was a child of the diaspora. But when he spoke to me, in 1968, about leaving Chile, this idea of belonging to a community of foreign exiles stirred within me a fear that came from vacant tables and broken mirrors.

I felt that my body was covered with a green layer of scales and bad omens. I felt cold when I heard the paper maps rustling in the hands of my parents. I didn't want to see anything new. I loved my country, its shores and

its melodic language like the sweet rippling rivers. Ye
I heard a voice that said: We will go to look for othe
islands, to surround ourselves with other seas.

My mother balanced herself within a dark and mag
ical circle, telling us that Jews lack a national identity
that we are the most orphaned and exiled people of th
earth. But I didn't want to be an orphan. I wanted to
have friends and to accompany them while they left flow
ers for the Virgins. I wanted to sit in the folded skirt
of the old shepherd who sweated in his heavy wooler
garments in the summer months.

Sometimes I used to hide in my pockets *milagros*
the little mass cards bearing colored pictures of the
saints. But I knew that Jewish girls didn't have saints to
protect them.

This time my best friends told me that I would
return to the land of the Hebrews. The word *Jew*
seemed too harsh, and not the least bit subtle. In fact
we were not going to Israel, the homeland of the Jews
but to the United States, the last stop on so many
immigrant trails of tears.

Once again, we prepared to depart. My mother car
ried a handful of dirt from the southern regions of
her childhood, and my father his skeletons, which
accompanied him on his nights of shadows. I, on the
other hand, did not know what to take with me. My cache
of possessions seemed like a depository of lost objects
Memory seemed to stick to me like a covered tattoo.
But I left with them, and accepted the condition of being

from somewhere else and from nowhere in particular.

In the evenings sometimes, I still wake up sweating, as my father does, and I don't find the maps or the suitcases, only the nightmares of being a traveler without a place to go. The experience of exile is like a sinister rainfall. No one recognizes my name or the fragrance of my skin and no one caresses me because I am alone in a place where no one even recognizes my voice. This is how the lost and ephemeral memories of exiles are.

Suddenly, the voice of a messenger or an angel tells me that memory is right here, that it is like a music box that only needs to be opened in order to begin the process of recall.

## Farewell to Chile

While we prepared for our trip to North America, we were living in unstable times filled with the doubts and anxieties of departure. In Chile my sister and brother and I had been happy. Our childhood was lived in all its plenitude, unfettered by schedules and unnecessary agendas. We enjoyed eating ice cream, having free time, and being with the ones we loved. My father, on the other hand, was worn-out and shocked by the constant accusations in the press against his character.

In Chile they denounced him for being an imperialist simply because he was receiving grants from the United States. Yet when he applied for residency in the United States, the U.S. Embassy investigated our family thoroughly, requesting an endless supply of documents and above all checking to see if any of us had ever had a police record. When they interviewed my father at the time he applied for a residency permit, the authorities asked him if he had ever thought about overthrowing the American government and if he had ever belonged to a communist organization. Curiously, although they had no way of knowing that he was a Jew, they did not ask whether or not he had ever been associated with the Nazi-sympathizers so prevalent in Chile. The bureaucrat asking him the questions was, of course, simply fulfilling his job. My father obtained residency for himself and the entire family. One evening in November we embarked on what has been, until now, our last pilgrimage.

I can only remember the night in all its deepness and enchantment. The hills were filled with early summer fragrances and it seemed impossible to touch the flower-covered domes of the soon-to-be abandoned trees. I gazed at the Andean cordillera and squinted. For the first time the range appeared tiny and lost, as if a weaver of dreams had built the receding peaks.

All of my schoolmates came to the airport dressed in their blue uniforms. Their faces reflected happiness and bewilderment. I didn't think about returns or absences. I wanted to remember them as they were. They gave me a record of the popular folk group, Bric a Brac, and they sang the song "Si vas para Chile" (If you are going to Chile). However, as I listened, I was also overwhelmed by something that seemed to tear its way deep into my soul, something that presaged the sadness of leaving everything behind and feeling foreign at all hours, of living on shifting and borrowed land.

This is how we came to America, the land of haste and solitary customs—an America whose memory did not belong to me.

## Nostalgia

From the nostalgia-laden past, we invent countries like dreams; we sketch false rivers, imagine certain aromas, and speak the language of the homeland as if it were a ring sealing love's alliances.

## Spanish Moss

Certain images prolong themselves in memory or in the wounds of all of the emigrants. Mine is of our arrival in the United States. We landed in Savannah, Georgia, worn out from our voyage across mountain ranges and seas, away from distant loves. A very dear friend of my father, the now-deceased entomologist Albert Perry, who presented me with a collection of butterflies and flies from the southern United States, greeted us at the gate. We climbed into one of those immense automobiles that we had only seen in North American movies. The car had three rows of seats, and was filled with blankets and bottles of Coca-Cola. It seemed like a friendly dwelling, and it transported us, like a self-assured mother, through the wide Savannah avenues.

As we traveled along the road, we saw beardlike presences swaying among the trees. They were thin tufts of hair that moved and whistled in the starry night. These forms hanging in the darkness were known as Spanish moss. I feared them because, like our new life, they were unpredictable and disturbing, like flames in the darkness of our beginnings.

## El Norte

When my father decided to leave Chile, he had called his friends in various places to help him find a job. This is how we ended up in Athens, Georgia, a pleasant city with smooth hills and ferns. At that time, I had not yet turned thirteen years old. I did not speak English and, more than anything else, I missed my Hebrew school.

Strangely, I have never written about my early experiences in the United States of America. It is only now, as I write about the lives of my parents, that I evoke the confusion of the Allende years, when we moved to the great North American continent, and the terror of the Pinochet years, when we realized that our exile would be permanent.

The experience of those first months and years in the United States continues to be disconsolate and ambiguous for me. It is only recently, now that nearly thirty years have passed, that I dare speak about Georgia–about the times when no one would talk to me in school because I was a Latina and a Jew; about the boy named Charlie who spat at me and made fun of my shortness, my clothing, and my fear of dogs.

All the happiness we had in Chile was left behind. My father's prestige and his immense laboratory were replaced by a small, sixth-floor room belonging to the Department of Zoology at the University of Georgia. Our house in Santiago, with its enormous welcoming terraces, its gardens of brilliant honeysuckle bushes and fruit trees, was only alive in our memories. In Georgia we leased a small house in a conservative neighborhood where the neighbors looked at us with suspicion. There, my mother and I would weep among the plastic chairs and empty rooms. It was a house deprived of the possibility of hearing laughter, where the smell of fried onions and garlic had been replaced by the sound of dogs barking. This was the legendary, colossal North America, and we felt so insignificant before the devastating solitude and remote riches.

We wrote letters constantly and cried frequently, until time made its wise pacts with a forced destiny. We assumed the posture of immigrants, a condition we felt especially in public places, every time we opened our mouths to say "Hi."

## A House of Exile

Do you remember, my mother would say, that forsaken house in the shade of the pine trees that would acquire a strange and foreign shape in the late afternoon? Do you remember, she would say, that empty house with the stained floors, with only a few extra chairs for absent guests? Do you remember that house in North America, where no one would knock at the door or come to sell us baked goods like the women in our old neighborhood did? That house without coriander smells?

I would tell my mother that, more than the empty house, I remember her burning and swollen eyes, sleepless as if they were forecasting dangers, and more distant than distance itself. I remember her voice amid the mist with its sobs and murmurs, and certain gestures approaching madness. More than the empty house, I remember my mother hugging me for endless hours during which her moist breath would confuse itself with mine. They were the salt-filled breaths of abandonment. She would say that here was where my father had brought us. The pain was very sharp, and we felt grief driving us into a corner like the pernicious shadow of death.

## The South

I had come from the southern tip of the world, but now I was in a region that was known as the "Deep South." For me, it was a south missing from the map, a place shrouded in fog that rose in the humidity of the pasturelands.

This was the south of tied-up voices, swamps, flying squirrels, and a sinister history of racism and bonfires. My first day at school I heard some children say: "Don't talk to her. She's a Jew and a Latina." They had also called me a Jew in the streets of Santiago and had laughed at my strange nose, but the matter of my being a Latina had never been spoken of in a derogatory way. It puzzled me very much because I did not speak Latin or descend from a Mediterranean race.

In a short while I discovered that I had come to the country of polls, classifications, and stereotypes created in order to justify continued abuses of power by the feudal landlords and the petty politicians. I had come to a country where everybody locked their doors at dusk.

## Folly

Sometimes I have wished that I looked like my mother, who has copper-toned skin and violet-colored eyes. My pale skin and blonde hair have always produced bewilderment and confusion in the United States. For example, people don't believe that I am Latin American or that I am Jewish. They also do not believe that my lineage is Austrian, and least of all that it is Russian. Many times I have heard people say, in front of me, how Jews are greedy and unbearable, how Hispanics are dirty and foolish. When I was a child, I would retreat into silence and pain. Now, with the face of an angel, I tell them that I am also Jewish and Latin American and that I don't have one foolish hair on my head.

## French Fries

Recalling our first days in America, I remember the french fries, the half-cooked beefsteak, and our empty house, where we waited for the mail from Chile and observed births, weddings, and deaths pass by from a distance, as if we were loyal spectators of an always foreign life.

## American Friends

My father came to North America, and in subtle ways they laughed at him—at his short height, his sparse hair and his accent. They discriminated against him with absurd jokes and low wages. In spite of this—and in spite of his history of exiles, his constant memory of foreign places and of a childhood spent in them, in spite of the prejudice and isolation—my father's life in the United States was professionally successful. He created great projects, especially in the field of biochemistry. I often heard him speak with passion about flies and vinchuca bugs. He also managed to bring many young Latin American students to the university who could easily fill up our house on those lazy Sunday afternoons in Athens, Georgia.

However, our true friends were in Chile. My father's colleagues here were never part of our life. My parents found it impossible to imagine hosting a formal dinner party, because there would not have been enough people to invite. And now that my father has retired after more than twenty-five years at the University of Georgia, he knows that he has many acquaintances but no soulmates.

Is this the condition of the foreigner—a kind of permanent exile, social as well as geographical? Perhaps, but I think that the concept of friendship in Latin America, Europe, and Asia is also very different from what it is in the United States, where even human relationships seem to be surrounded by a mediocre consumerism and a poverty of the spirit, where time spent in comradeship and conversation becomes nothing more than a disturbance. Here everything is measured, everything is by the hour. Even friendship is often a commercial transaction.

In the United States, I cannot remember any party with wide, smiling faces.

## Prejudice in the Exact Sciences

My father always talks about the shady secrets of the universe, of the ethical miserliness of certain scientists, their pettiness and hidden prejudices. During his first stay in the United States, in 1953, my father worked at the NIH. There he always felt deficient in mathematics because of his "Third World" preparation. Therefore, in the evenings he took classes at a nearby university.

The professor was an African-American from Howard University. When the students learned this, the enrollment quickly diminished from the initial twenty students to only three. This was my father's first encounter with racism in universities in the United States. When he returned fifteen years later, he would learn much more about this disturbing subject.

My father learned that racism within the academy was subtle but deliberately consistent. In the exact sciences there were terrible prejudices against Latin American scientists, who were thought to be indolent, disorganized, and unsanitary in their research methods. According to my father, these attitudes have existed from the time he first came to the United States to the present day, in spite of considerable efforts to change them by some individuals of good will. There are prejudices not only against foreign scientists, but also against native-born scientists from different cultural backgrounds and from different regions of the country. Once he met a man who would not associate with people who had not graduated from M.I.T. What could my father possibly say to this man, having himself graduated from the University of Chile?

My father often commented on the lack of ethics in scientific research in the United States. Racism is often a factor in the unethical scientific practices. My father talks about a conference where a very respected immunologist applauded the practice of injecting parasites into South American Indians contaminated with other parasites to see how they would react to the procedure. He felt there was no point in explaining to the subjects of this study what was being done to them; they were, after all, only Indians.

Today it has been revealed that in the 1920s in Tuskegee, Alabama, a group of African-Americans infected with syphilis was left untreated so as to serve as a control to another group treated with penicillin. They believed that they were being treated for their disease, and did not know that their suffering was being rationalized in the name of science. It has been revealed, too, that during the period of the Cold War, American authorities carried out experiments on the effects of nuclear radiation on unwitting adults and children; these continued in complete secrecy until the decade of the 1970s.

Such revelations do not seem to have any effect on people's prejudices. It is still those of us from the "Third World" who are accused of coming from a land of savages.

## Human Rights

Our exile was dominated by an obsession with human rights violations in Chile and in neighboring countries. Week by week, we tracked the record of assassinations, tortures, and disappearances that continued throughout the Pinochet regime. We scanned the newspapers for rare mentions of the ongoing terror in our homeland, and when we opened the treasured letters that arrived from Chile, our sense of joy was always accompanied by a touch of dread. Sometimes they contained the names of friends, colleagues, or acquaintances—even a young classmate of mine—followed by that heartbreaking word: *disappeared.*

As a scientist, my father was particularly disturbed by any violation of human rights executed in the name of the so-called good-will sciences. There have been many cases of indigenous peoples being injected with microbes, bacteria, and viruses in order to determine their immunity (or lack of immunity) to disease. Scientists talk about these studies as if the indigenous people were foreign and distant objects that do not belong to human or divine spheres.

Although these scientists most often descended from the north in search of pliable subjects to the south, Latin American researchers have not been above visiting these tortures on their countrymen. It is a well-known fact that in northern Chile there was a community stricken by a high incidence of goiter-related illnesses. In the 1950s, a group of scientists from the University of Chile exposed the citizens to radiation, causing premature death in many of them. An attempt was made to bring this group of researchers to trial. However, they were released "without impunity," like the agents of Pinochet—including the doctors-turned-tortures—who received amnesty in 1991 in spite of the fact that they had violated the human rights of thousands.

The most notorious case of science mixing with torture is that of Josef Mengele, the German doctor who carried out all sorts of experiments on Jewish prisoners during World War II, especially with children who were twins. After the war, he lived as an aged fugitive in various places in South America—in Bolivia, in Brazil, and perhaps even Chile.

## Perú

My father, too, sometimes travelled as a scientist to the remote regions of South America. But his work there, like his soul, was guided by a deep humanity. Several times he visited Perú to provide training to Peruvian scientists and to give advice on ongoing research in tropical medicine.

My father grew to love this Andean country, with its remote villages, hidden between the mountains and the jungle, and its indigenous cultures, so rich in tradition yet so besieged by prejudice, poverty, and disease. He loved the ruggedness of its people and the secret lines of history.

In Perú my father loved everybody who was eclipsed by the destiny of their skin color, but more than anything, he loved the dispossessed, those who passed the night in the silence of death and diaspora. He worked months, centuries, and luminous instants to discover medicines and auspicious herbs that would cure the evils of poverty on the skin of crestfallen men. He did all this because the Indians, like all human beings, deserved happiness and time to enjoy the rituals of their ancestors.

Perú, a slender and somnambulant strip of land; Perú, dwelling between the stories of weavers and lost stars. Sonorous and sad Perú, pierced by the slippery and distant Andean wind like a knife circling the deepness of the night and its sadness. In our family stories, Perú stands like the infamy and beauty of a memory lost and darkened by hunger.

## Contemplating Choices

My father would sometimes ask what motivated an individual to dedicate himself or herself to scientific research. He believed that to be a good scientist, a person must have a calling, an avid curiosity, a need to know why things worked in a certain way and not in another; be of at least average intelligence; and not be interested in material gain. I know that my father had all these qualities.

Still, my father faults himself for one quality he lacked: he says that when he chose to pursue the research he loved, he did not have a sense of economic responsibility toward his family. In a country like the United States, scientists earn enough to live well and take care of their families. In many "Third World" countries, on the other hand, scientific research is exclusively a profession of the well-to-do. Researchers' salaries there have always been kept low, in order to prevent "adventurers" incited by greed from entering such a rich and exclusive field. The years my father worked in Chile were ones of constant sacrifice, because the money he received for his research could not be considered a good income.

At a recent reunion given in his honor, my father had the pleasure of meeting with two of his colleagues from medical school in Chile: Boris Rotman, who was professor emeritus at Brown University, and Basil Fine, the South African student my father had known from England who had abandoned research in order to practice medicine in Boston. He also visited with his grandchildren, Joseph and Sonia. Among the various generations at the party, my father saw his past, present, and future.

At the time, my father told me he realized that the decision to emigrate to the United States had been beneficial in many ways. Undoubtedly it was so from an economic point of view, because in North America he had eventually achieved a level of income that would never have been possible in Chile. But what mattered most to my father—what made the money valuable—was the opportunity to educate his children, who had all become successful in their respective careers. The pain of his own journeys had guaranteed his family's future.

Now we feel more secure in our new country. Even though people still ask us where we are from when they notice our accent, it no longer bothers us so much. Our children speak English like natives, and they don't have to face the distrust that my parents faced as immigrants from the South.

## The Wall, 1972

My father and I, wanderers, explorers of distant stars, roam through Israel. The wind moans, invents and tempts forgetfulness. It enters behind the hills and the masks of history so that the dead can listen and so that oblivion will not be a swarm of smooth stones. We walk through the *shuk,* and it seems to us as if we were in a Mexican marketplace or in some lost neighborhood in Santiago, Chile. Here in Israel, they say that we are Sephardic Jews because we are from Latin America; it does not matter that we originally came from Russia or Poland. For the Israelis, we are Sephardim because we speak Spanish. It is interesting how even the land of Israel transfigures our identity. Nevertheless, we navigate across these rocks that seem to kindle with the steps of each traveller, and beyond the silence, my father and I find a way to talk with God.

I approach the Wailing Wall on the women's side. Confusing my face with its shadows, I delight in the smell of wet herbs arising from its surface. As I kiss the wall, it seems as if I were kissing all of my relatives, all the prodigal sons and daughters who died in the countless wars. A woman, upset by the fear of solitude, lets slip between the darkened cracks of the wall a message to God as well as a message to me, because I am a witness of her history, which is also mine. I look at her and see a destitute woman with numbers on her arms and children lost in all the battles of all the vanquished. I then return through those streets of beggars and phantoms while the sounds of prayers in Hebrew and Arabic fill the air as the Sabbath begins. My father and I meet again. He had looked for me from afar and stayed at the wall for a long time, even though he didn't leave behind a message for God. As he hugs me, his voice glistens, as if some presence had touched him, as if the secrets of the wind had reached him from the whispers of the dead here in the golden and obscure city of Jerusalem.

## Mario

The language spoken in our home was and continues to be Spanish. There was no pressure or desire to maintain a perfect-sounding English. On the contrary, we all wanted to speak our language, to remember our words. Spanish was our most exquisite link with the land that we inhabited, where at dawn we imagined the Andean cordillera at our feet, seeming to approach the shores of our dreams. Spanish became the language in which we maintained an inventory of our melancholy. With words we took stock of our ancestry and of the possibility of recall.

My brother Mario came to America when he was very little and had not yet begun to talk. In his passport they declared him "single, illiterate, and jobless." At school his teachers were very anxious because of Mario's profound silence. But suddenly, one day, in a perfect Georgia accent, he told a disobedient child to "sit and keep still." This is how my brother Mario established his identity using the English language.

For many years, our immediate family had been made up of four people: my parents, my sister, and me. For economic reasons, my parents had no desire to expand our family. My father was surprised when a friend told him that the birth of a son had made him feel different and fulfilled. My father always believed that children should be loved for who they were and not because of their gender. However, eleven years after the births of my sister and me, my parents had a son whom they named Mario, like the Italian prince my mother read about in old encyclopedias.

Mario was an extremely quiet, solitary, and independent child. Through my parents' common sense, he was educated with grace. Although my sister and I had received half of our education at the Hebrew school in Santiago, my brother did not have a similar opportunity because at that time in Athens, Georgia, there were no Hebrew schools. Mario did, however, attend classes to prepare himself for his Bar Mitzvah.

As the date of his Bar Mitzvah approached, my father had to go to Israel and decided to bring all of us with him. While there, my father wanted the rabbi who had married him, and who had later moved to Israel, to officiate at Mario's Bar Mitzvah. However, the rabbi flatly refused, saying that he only officiated at ceremonies in his congregation and not for others. My father's friend Al Perry told him to talk to any one of the rabbis near the Wailing Wall because they officiated at Bar Mitzvahs, and although Mario was not quite thirteen years old, Al Perry convinced a rabbi that he was the right age and that his great moment had arrived.

Mario entered the area where the ceremony would take place together with other young boys, all Yemenite Jews. The women, including my mother and I, had to remain behind a barrier in the distance. Male relatives and friends stood with the boys. Individuals from the most distinguished families had access to the area at the front of the room, but the rest, those from the desert, the wanderers and Sephardim, were only permitted to stand in the rear. My brother was there in the back, a lost Chilean Jew who lived in Georgia, possessing no great title of nobility except for his innocence and dubious faith.

Later my father told me that he wasn't aware of the irony of the situation until many years had passed. His son, who had no Jewish education, had officially been declared an adult in the Jewish community—and in Israel, no less—while his two daughters, who speak fluent Hebrew and can quote from the Talmud at will, were never given Bat Mitzvahs. When the ceremony ended, we wanted to give my brother an exquisitely sumptuous feast. One can imagine how surprised we were when Mario told us that all he wanted was a hamburger with french fries, which proved to us that while he might be a Jew he was surely the only true gringo in our family.

My father tells me that he still thinks his friend was wrong. Now that he has three children, one of them a boy, he loves them all equally.

## Passover

Coming from the southern tip of the world, we retain a strange sense, in the United States, that the seasons are all wrong–they are backwards, reversed. In the north, we celebrate Passover at the beginning of spring. This year my son repeats the four questions in English as I remember repeating them in Spanish in the open courtyard of my school, where all of the children would meet to celebrate this holiday of liberation and the beginning of fall, while smelling the almonds and chestnuts as if coming out of a dream. Sephardic families with children who looked like wizards and musicians would come from very far away bearing baskets of fruit and nuts. They told us that it was very nice of us to conserve the Ladino songs because they had an exquisite Spanish flavor. This is what I most remember about Passover: the Ladino songs in a school filled with Israeli teachers who were survivors of the Holocaust and who tried always to be pioneers as they also recovered the laments of their past.

I think of myself as a Latin American Jewish woman

with an affinity for warm Ladino melodies, stories of Moroccan Jewish sultanas and of Queen Esther, who saved her people through faith and song, and whose courage is remembered through the generations.

I am happy that my children celebrate Passover and think about the flight from Egypt, and I am happy that they accept the diaspora as something that belongs to them. We are a mixture of free peoples. We are a people of God. I think of Jerusalem and its cupolas and of the gentle dawns of Toledo, where centuries ago, children sang the same songs that I heard in the Hebrew school of Santiago, Chile. Today I still sing these melodies to my children in an America that is so far north and yet still Hispanic.

## Letters

Seated by my side with an old and distant gaze, my father asks me if the letters have arrived–those letters from Chile that foreshadow the happiness of newlyweds and the peace of the dead, those letters that we have waited for, daily, for nearly thirty years. They are letters from distant friends, who talk to him about his dilapidated laboratory and about our house, now inhabited by the noises made by the footsteps of others.

People in exile adjust to foreign landscapes. They hold onto letters with much eagerness and passion–a passion for memory, for past experiences, and for usurped time. I contemplate my father waiting for the letters. He has the gaze of an absent man who interrogates beings from other spheres, from countries close to an also distant sky. Exile is a state of crude recalling, of being and not being anywhere, of waiting for the arrival of the familiar in foreign places, of feeling oneself always remote.

## Uncertain Travelers

Exile is roaming from country to country, inventing new languages and remembering distant ones. But for the Jews, exile has been simply a way of living. It has been a time for creating walls and interior dwellings in order to preserve memory in its tenuous blanket of mist. This is why Jews can live anywhere in the world. They are from everywhere and nowhere. They adapt to streets and landscapes and wait for better times and future seasons. In spite of everything, however, it is difficult for me to understand those who say that the ghetto was paradise. Their words remind me of the statements made by certain Chilean mothers, who contented themselves with recovering little plastic bags containing the bones of their disappeared children.

Exile will always accompany us; it has become our permanent, obsessive condition. My family dreams of an almost dislocated and imaginary Chile, but after a while we have come to desire this piece of North American sky, and to love certain people who dared to speak to us.

## Living in Translation

Our life in the United States has always balanced itself between the frontiers of return and the misty memory of flight. When we arrived in Athens, Georgia, we bought few pieces of furniture because we were always hoping to return to Chile. We talked about our country, wrote letters, and dreamed about the cordillera, knowing that we lived too far away from it. We ate our tasty foods seasoned with garlic and herbs, our fresh vegetables, and never tried to become part of a culture that was so foreign and distant from our own, where people greeted each other with caution, where time was a slender border of fear, and where no one dared to ask about the health of the sick. We lived in a borrowed zone, knowing that at any moment we might have to leave, as if we were waiting for the end of the war, the surrender of our furniture, and the glorious return to life.

Chile's military dictatorship lasted almost twenty years. We lost friends who disappeared clandestinely and who now have disappeared from the memory of those who knew them. We missed births and funerals. Our identity lay confused, suspended between imaginary and real borders. We lived in translation.

Now my father and all of us reside in a type of atemporal land, in a region lost between the memory of what was and what we have fabricated across distances. We are Jews without a country. Every day we learn other languages and live in borrowed houses. I believe that if they were to blindfold us, we would find the road home.

## Journeys Home

Our return to Chile feels genuine because no one looks at us with suspicion in the vestibule of the offices of those ominous international police. No one looks at us as if we were dangerous strangers because we carry books of poetry and compromising pencils. The age of terror in Chile has ended. Now they say that we are in a democracy, celebrating reconciliation and love. We do not fully believe it. We know that when a former dictator and torturer can become a senator, the nation's victory is an imperfect one. But we know that in a wounded world, we must accept even imperfect victories as a cause of celebration.

Still, we question why we have chosen to return. We can no longer return and kiss all of our family members and friends who have died and those who crossed the cordillera and decided not to come back. The years of the military dictatorship robbed us of speech and of the possibility of wonder. They created an ominous silence and also prevented us from being close to our loved ones, grandparents and parents. We grew up without our family and friends. The dictatorship obliged us to flee, and to become entangled in a silence even more complex and heart-rending than that suffered by those who had remained inside. At least in

Chile one could talk in groups of two or three people, repeat certain statements in the ear and kiss like dragonflies. In exile we were alone, foreign to the foods and celebrations. We had no one with whom to share those afternoons of happiness, lying on the grass and intoxicating ourselves with a cup of tea, or those end-of-the-year parties with the yellow lanterns. We were solitary beings, gazing through a window that wasn't ours toward trees that didn't belong to us, speaking borrowed languages in an empty living room, alone and heartbroken. Now we return, if only to visit certain graves and places where our shadows passed in order to give our ancestors something to drink.

## The Flavors of Memory

During many years of exile in North America, we lived by recreating the flavors of memory. We missed the succulent fruits of Chile—peaches, grapes, and valley figs—and pined for those light and silky dishes. The food, like poetry, conversation, and table wines, was part of a link that each day became more fragile and remote. Nonetheless, we always felt that Chile was forever present in our minds, like a compass guiding us in our new lives.

In sad nights forged in insomnia, my father and I imagined the rhythms of certain stars and we sketched the constellations that pointed the way home. Now I also return, and in this voyage I approach regions of uncertainty. I am and am not from these parallels. I am also that little girl who marvelled before the noise of imaginary sea horses and goblins.

I return to Chile to make sure that people will still recognize me and tell me that I am the daughter of Dr. Agosín, for this encounter with the past calms me. I return to Chile, but this time I also realize that not even the past, not even our nostalgia for that which was, pertains to us now. We are destined to repeat incessantly the gestures of all wandering peoples. We will always be foreign inhabitants, prepared for flight, always from somewhere else.

*My brother Mario with my father in Jerusalem at his Bar Mitzvah, 1970.*

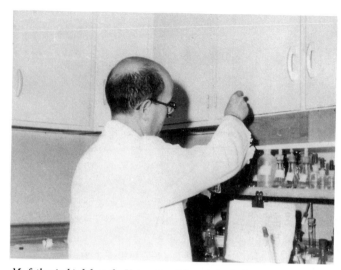

*My father in his lab at the University of Georgia in the late 1970s.*

*My parents with me at my wedding, Athens, Georgia, 1977.*

*My sister Cynthia, me, my mother, and my brother Mario at my parents'
home in Athens, Georgia, in the early 1980s.*

# MEMORY'S PLACE

## Dream Maker

I did not search for memory among the cloudy monuments or the cathedrals that had been synagogues, resembling obscure grottoes. Nor did I search for the names of certain streets where the dead sisters still drink the water. I devoted myself to searching for memory as if it were a gathered breath in a notebook held by some small, adorned hands. I searched for memory as if I were someone opening my eyes for a moment to glimpse the signs of unspoken words.

Memory and I were like the rings of ancient impassive trees, united among all the longings and possibilities. I felt the pulse of memory, like a great heart that lived between its beats, overcast and transparent, diaphanous and nocturnal, and I paused to listen to its voice. Sometimes it was clear, like a howl in the night, and other times it seemed to obscure itself, like a thin, luminous layer in the water's depths or the sound of the foliage on windswept days.

Memory and I travelled together. Nothing disturbed us, neither the abyss nor rustlings of death behind the shadows of the traversed cities. I learned to listen to her.

Weeping, I accepted her invitation and crossed over paths of damp stones. Now I am here, assisted by her.

As I write this story, I begin to smooth the threads of memory, to weave a fabric of words, to shape them into a cloak that will protect me from the cold.

## Memory in Her Carriage of Mist

Memory approaches in her carriage of mist. She is agile, dancing over the smoke of all time, wearing her hood of ashes. Memory watches over me, and sometimes when I think that I am carrying the signs of death, she only asks that I not forget her. She is a cautious lady, remembering certain moments and recording them in the great book of all history.

In the book of my father's memory I have toyed with certain chapters and invented others; I have slightly avenged myself of death's subtle talons so as to retrieve life from infinite, depthless time. While I write, I know that I am a woman who is both a Chilean and a Jew, a woman whose language has experienced many voyages and exiles, and who, like Scheherazade, tells and sings this story to save her own life. I am a descendent of all those who fled silently through the forests or suffered inside the barbed wire of the camps. I am a member of the disenchanted generation that lost its sense of wonder and filled the cemeteries with nameless bodies, the generation of the disappeared. Yet I am also one of those who still wish to invent faith from chaos.

I write this great and small memoir and know that among the ashes of Auschwitz and also on the remote Quiriquina Islands, where Chilean political prisoners lived and died, the smoke of the dancing figures, of the ghosts and phantoms, rises in the air like a great clamorous being that wants to stir itself up even more. In the distance, as I write, stand a woman who perished in the Holocaust and a woman who survived, a disappeared woman and the mother of a disappeared daughter. They are washing the clothes of the dead, like sleepwalkers whose faces fill with rivers and names.

I write these memoirs and know that I am among the dancing spirit navigators who travel on fragile vessels of the soul extending from Jerusalem to Santiago. We have made our journeys, with suffering and with love, in order to be here today and to say the words that no one ought to forget.

I write my father's story and I put my own life in order. My memory intensifies before the sorrow of the rubble and the flames. I write, but sometimes do not recognize myself. Solitude and fear have lacerated my face, but I am here. I like to imagine myself bringing gardenias to the Wailing Wall in Jerusalem and to the Memorial of the Disappeared in Santiago.

## Lost Dominions

I write these memories of my father, which also accompany mine. I reconstruct and arrange the signs, the crestfallen and drowsy stars. This is my vocation; I am like an alchemist in love with the alphabet and its gestures and with the methodical rhythm of memory. I write and reinvent and search for, with heart-rending tenderness, the words that will draw me closest to the truth. All memory is a lost dominion, all history, a memory to recall.

I begin to write this book of memories during the winter of 1995, when the world is remembering Anne Frank, Auschwitz, and the railroad tracks that led with certainty to the petrified silence of a Dantesque hell. My father survived to pass on his memories to me; by some accidents of fate, he was not among those who made that journey of no return. But I know that he could have been one of them.

## Babylon

I am a Babylonian of forget-me-nots. My tongue is for speaking but also for distributing caresses and accompanying my children on the voyages of memories. I am a Jewish Chilean writer who was born by chance in North America because my father, a Jewish scientist born in France and nationalized in Chile, decided to cross oceans, invent and tell tales in other lands. We are the offspring of a line of mute and silent wanderers. We are Jews recovering time and speaking in borrowed zones. Being Chilean and Jewish is an ambiguity more than a conflict. There are places where Jews get together to name and collect stories of smoke, where Jews and non-Jews visit their dead, leaving behind two or three stones for all the returns.

## Sea Voyages

I return to Chile, and between the paths, beyond the mist, I also search for clues of my father's presence, for the faces of those who knew him as a child and intuited his oddness, his strange way of gazing that was only a disguised game to protect himself from his premature baldness and shyness.

Amid the fog that sprinkles my face with a fine mist, in a wooden boat built by Greek emigrant fishermen, I navigate through my country, which resembles a flower petal stretched out over the seas. On the boat, which also plays a part in the small destiny of my voyages, I meet the children of Germans who seemed to have emerged from the old photographs and magazines of the thirties. As they talk with me, I realize that they themselves have erased certain histories and confused the dates when their ancestors came to Chile. Some say that it was in the late 1930s and others say that it was more than 150 years ago. I also learn that many of them knew my father because they happened to come from the same city, Quillota.

During the voyage I keep thinking about life as a fragile, incongruous thread that we all weave, taking down certain stories, creating tapestries, opening and shutting windows. They, like me, have assembled together certain memories so as to calm themselves before death, knowing that in this last corner of the world they hold memories that are like broken and transparent mirrors.

Some of the Germans who travel with me, in spite of having been born in my country and having lived in Chile for over fifty years, identify with Germany, proudly speaking to one another in their bittersweet language. They seem like privileged visitors on this boat of middle-class Chileans, whose manners and lexicon have nothing to do with the people who travel on the big European transatlantic liners. Subtly, without a desire to humiliate, the German passengers reveal that they believe themselves to be sovereigns. They look upon the small and indigenous crew with an attitude of paternalism and they talk to them with a light, arrogant tone.

These same Germans are familiar with the Agosín tailor shop whose proprietor was my grandfather, "the Jew." And of course, they know that my father could not go to private school because the Salesian priests had not accepted him. Ingenuously, I think that perhaps in the square they could have exchanged greetings with my father and played together as children. But these are only my fantasies. These gentlemen frequented the closed circles and met behind locked doors. My father never went to visit them in their immense mansions because those places were always prohibited to Jews.

I travel with them on this radiant sea, with its rippling tides like silk bracelets floated on the waves, past shores of ice and forests. I think of the unspoken questions, those never-asked questions: What did the parents of that Berlin gentleman who was now eating with me do at the time of the war? What was his mother doing while she saw the deprived, subjugated, and broken Jews approach the village railway stations and depart toward the chambers of certain death, where they would become waves of human ash?

We voyage past the immensity of this crystalline ice. My country overwhelms me with its beauty, stretched out like a reclining queen. Chile has some of the most inhospitable territories in the world and some of the most generous zones. There are strange characters living there, beings immersed in nostalgia and sadness. The jews of Chile still live in an atmosphere of isolation and distrust, while German presence remains strong. Germans are the preferred tourists and the principal characters in all of the stories having to do with the military in Chile. They appear as the most important colonists, occupying seats of honor at presidential meetings. Jews occupy the back seats, the invisible and silent places. Only a few books, seldom read, tell the story of the Jews of Chile. Recently, a center of Judaic Studies in Buenos Aires was bombed, erasing all traces of written memory, of the books of God.

## Intolerance

Intolerance is terror in the face of Otherness. Intolerance produced the pogroms that drove my ancestors from Russia. Intolerance of a slightly different kind reigned fifty years later in the countries at the southern tip of Latin America under the culture of fear, where ideologies grew that encouraged people to cross the street in order to avoid an encounter with a persecuted friend.

We should not be reluctant to think that the person who shouted "Land!" when Christopher Columbus's fragile ship touched American soil might have been a Jew fleeing the Spanish Inquisition. The Jews have always come to America, to escape the burnings and the tortured bodies, the ashes and the disillusionment. "This is how I also came," says my father. He left Marseilles with German measles and was hidden beneath his mother Raquel's skirts so that they would not throw him into the sea. Now he resides in another exile in the northern hemisphere, escaping other dangers.

## Survivors

Not being from anywhere, inventing boundaries and living outside of them, has been our stigma and our legacy. It is a legacy that gives us a certain clarity of vision. We have come to understand that the hatred and intolerance inherent in anti-Semitism is a universal phenomenon that does not affect only Jews.

Many Jews who survived the Holocaust have dedicated their lives to talking about memory and faithfully documenting events in the hope that others will learn from this experience. Sadly, their efforts are often proved futile. One need only look at the terrified faces of the women of Bosnia or read about the burning churches in the southern United States to realize that the lessons have not been learned, and that human beings, instead of trying to comprehend others, still destroy everything that they do not understand.

## Memories Buried and Burned

During the years of the military dictatorship in Chile, there were countless murders of "dissidents" and impoverished peasants, who were then buried in undisclosed places. The crime committed in the small peasant community of Lonquén was truly indescribable. An entire peasant family of twelve was buried alive in an immense oven. This incident, of course, recalls the crematoria of Auschwitz, the ashes and the skin of the dead, the smoke and the silence. During the years of the military dictatorship, the smoke blinded us. The silence shrouded us with a great sinister cape. Fear shaved our souls.

I remember how, during our visits to Chile for family reunions, the lights were turned off and the windows sealed. Permission had to be granted by the authorities in order to have a gathering of more than five people at home. This makes me think about the history of the

Jews in Europe and in the Middle East, who sealed their windows when they lit the sabbath candles.

Sometimes my father and I go back further into the secret passages of that history, to the Inquisition and the *autos-da-fé*, where Jews burned in silence with the name of God on their singed lips. This same phenomenon draws us closer to Chile in the seventies and to the fateful persecution of the "Other," that strong desire to exterminate other ways of being, other gazes. We also remember that the neighbors, those individuals who had been friendly and hospitable years before, refused to open their doors, turning against us in a glorious desire to persecute and assassinate the Other.

And to think that all this occurred only a short while ago. We all were and are accomplices of a history that repeats itself, in which new concentration camps exist and the thin and pale figure of Anne Frank appears to us at night.

In 1933 the Nazis burned the books of the intellectual Jews of Berlin. I remember that in Chile in 1972, my grandfather decided to burn my father's medical books, especially those written by Freud, the volumes that reflected my father's great passion for psychiatry. The pyre of books reached into the deepest areas of our house and neighborhood. These books were considered seditious by Pinochet. They would have represented a danger to our relatives in Chile had they been found by the secret police. In 1973 and 1974 pyres of books continued burning throughout the entire country, now desolate and solitary, whistling in the dark, lost and naked before the intolerance and torture that were killing it from within.

## Fascism in Chile, 1995

Fascism in Chile, as in so many European countries, continues surfacing with an illogical strength. Pro-Nazi companies are once again investing in this country of false, confused, and solitary illusions. In the bookstores of the upper-class neighborhoods of Santiago, the bestsellers of the moment are new editions of *The Protocols of the Elders of Zion* and *Mein Kampf,* and at the public cemetery thousands of students from the elite neighborhoods of Santiago gather to remember the anniversary of Hitler's birth with the same devotion that they exhibit when they remember Pinochet.

Anti-Semitism in Chile is now just as prevalent and furtive as it was in the 1940s during the war years, and the German presence looms forth, creating an energy that moves toward all sectors of the imaginary Chilean landscape. It is an energy embedded in fascism, in the idea of white supremacy, and in the negation of the indigenous and the Jew.

## Puerto Aguirre, 1995

My husband and I are on a cruise ship in the lake region of Chile. We like the hushed rustling movements of this vessel of smooth, blonde wood. In the dining area, the passengers take stock of one another with their gaze. I feel very shy and don't know exactly where I fit in, for I speak perfect Spanish, yet I look like a foreigner. In the United States I look like a gringa, but I speak English with a foreign accent. Everywhere I go I am an anomalous and anonymous being, an outsider and stranger just like my father, who was told that he had a French and Yiddish accent even though he never spoke Yiddish and he was only three years old when he left Marseilles.

When they inquire about my origins, I tell them that I was raised in Chile, but that because of the fascist dictatorship, my family settled permanently in the United States. Then they look at me, more confused than ever, and ask the sly, age-old question: "And what school did you attend, my child?" When I tell them it was the Hebrew Institute, I see them smoothly raise their eyebrows and say, "Of course, you are Hebrew." They don't dare say *Jew,* because this word is too strong for them to articulate, but all the same, I hear them murmur, "Oh, so she is Jewish."

## Auschwitz, 1995

The ghosts of the dead return to the place where nothing blossoms, where the barbed wire rises in the clamor of a distance, where the nights are indistinguishable from the days. They are here with their split-open memories, their torn clothing, and their sorrow immersed in the void. There are no flowers or brides in the Auschwitz fields. The voices of the dead children are carried by the winds. Behind the voices there can be heard the steps of the guards. They say that this is the most sterile desert on the planet: Auschwitz. Even the name fills me with a perverse tremor. But we are here, and we do not turn away when we pass by the haunted barracks and the empty crematoria, all the places filled with bats and the ashes of dead women and hair that resembles sleepwalking algae.

Then I see her. Her name is Emma or Adela, and she holds a sepia-colored photograph lacerated by smoke. Burning with love, she caresses her photograph and says, "This is all that I have left of my family." She is like the women in Buenos Aires, in the Plaza de Mayo amid the mist, who raise a photograph and say very softly, "This is all that I have left of my family."

So much dust, so many bonfires. I also return with a worm-eaten photograph and ask myself, Why did I survive? Where did I come from? Where is the true house of God?

## Wellesley, 1995

Like peace-bearing omens, the light and winged snowflakes begin to fall from a sky that resembles a blanket of ashes. Sheltered within the heaviness of winter, we begin to remember the dead—our ancestors in Russia or in Auschwitz, our grandparents in Quillota and all the disappeared friends, buried in some public cemetery in a common grave or perhaps on the prison island, in the north among the dunes and implacable sun.

The victims no longer have names. Only those who loved them invoke their memories. But strangely, even these memories often turn to the executioners, who capture our interest almost more than the victims do. Is it because we identify with them? Is it because they awaken in us feelings of pity and curiosity and shared guilt? Or merely because they remain here with us, on the same side of the threshold of torture and death? The dead have stopped speaking; their bodies and souls have fearlessly crossed the threshold. Sometimes we try to humanize the victims with pictures that we show to others. Yet they remain buried beneath the layers of snow and sand, or toss and turn in the ocean swells. It is so difficult coming to terms with the fact that they were mutilated, dismembered, decapitated, and burned. It is impossible to understand the victims because we have not suffered the same tortures.

Memory is dense and filtered in this ambiguous, nebulous century, where obscurity and opacity predominate. This morning, it is snowing in New England. I am so far away from my parents and my imagined country, further away than the dead.

## Memoirs of the Living

We write the memoirs of the living so as not to leave behind the dead, so that we will not feel them slipping away from our breath and from the pulse of life, and so that the dead can finally sing. We write about our ancestors to defy death's certain embrace. Nothing remains of the Agosíns with the uncertain surnames who remained in Odessa or St. Petersburg. All that is left are cities among the rubble and neighborhoods with maimed children. However, everything as well as nothing remains of them–their footsteps, the photographs beyond the murky sepia tints, the traces of their slow walks through cities that still vibrate with the rhythm of life, the burned books. Most of this is lost because memory is nothing more than a voyage taken to the past in order to repair a room of broken mirrors.

My father, Moisés Agosín, is the last descendent of those navigators and tailors from Odessa who journeyed from Istanbul to Marseilles and eventually found refuge on lost Chilean shores. Sometimes his words embrace and cover me as if I were once again that eight-year-old girl who asked him for God's correct address. Both his hair and hands join with mine, connecting all of the routes of his journeys. I contemplate God, the world, and words through his story, and know that he has survived, has told his tale, and has not let himself be silenced by the muted histories.

These are the threads of memory: to tell and return

to the well-trodden paths of a boy named Moshka, who was born in Marseilles to Russian parents who spoke Turkish but came to the coasts of South America where they took refuge, immersed in the professions of cloth and medicine and with a love of life.

I am writing this book entitled *Always from Somewhere Else* because this is the ontological condition of navigating Jews, who live in borrowed regions but remain faithful followers of memory and of the great book of life that perhaps is the book of God.

## Fugitives

Exiles and fugitives like us are accustomed to returning to the beloved and imaginary motherland to visit the dead more than the living. We approach the lost dominions of roots and earth. My father and I visit the small, sun-bleached cemetery of Belloto, located between the cities of Quillota and Viña del Mar. While there, my father confesses to me that his father obsessively argued with God. He had a profound conflict with Him.

My grandparents never talked about Russia in Chile. They never talked about their family or friends. At home my grandfather even avoided speaking in the language of his ancestors, except in times of sorrow and nostalgic reminiscence. My grandmother, on the other hand, prayed in Russian and sometimes whispered in the little Yiddish that she had learned from other fugitives in Marseilles.

My father always asks himself where he came from and who his relatives were; this desire to want to know is one of the things that obsesses him. He has always suspected that Agosín is an invented name, a name that must have surfaced in the ambiguous and imaginary channels between Odessa and Turkey, travel-worn like the glass bottles bearing messages across the seas.

When my grandmother was preparing for the ritual of death, my father asked her if Agosín was really our name. She looked at him aghast, shook her head with the grief of those lacking direction, and said, "Moisés, your name is fine, but it isn't the name of your father." These were the last words softly spoken by my grandmother Raquel, the beautiful cigarette-maker from Odessa who sang in Russian and Turkish and who recited poems in French to drive away sorrow.

## Returns

All returns are premonitory signs, omens. We visit the cemeteries and gather stones from the river for dead friends. My father wishes to visit his school companion, René Christen, who defended him from Arabs and Nazis when they were both medical students, and who teased him about his outdated clothes and dusty shoes. He is told that René died a week before, on a misty summer morning. My father mourns René and crosses the seasons of memory, the alchemies of recall. He imagines certain dreams and the spring parties at

the student union. For the first time, he decides to pol-
ish his shoes.

## The Past

Jews have always yearned for the past, for stories
beyond the photographs of sepia-coated times, obscured
in the shadows of disquieting smoke. They are vagabonds
travelling through the invisible zones of memory. Jews
have always searched for the images beyond love and
the gas chambers.

My father carries the photographs of his parents
like a talisman of cloudy memories.

## The Collector

My father was never a collector of strange objects,
nor was he a materialist. Above all else he enjoyed under-
stated elegance and melodies like epiphanies. Among
his most prized possessions were the portrait of his mother, Raquel, when she was a cigarette-roller at the little
factory in Odessa and his first fly collection, sent to him
from England. My father intuited absences. He knew
that the cadences of love and misfortune never belonged
to him and that they were impossible to store because
everything was ephemeral and impalpable.

## The Names of the Dead

In spite of our often violent and sorrowful history, Jews worry more about life than about death. This is why even in life they repeat the names of the dead. It is why my children are named after my grandparents, and the children of my children's children will be named after me. Is this not a way to make life expand and remain inconclusive and exist perpetually in the present?

## Yom Kippur

There is so much silence in the air and the sky is dense like an unfinished melody; such is the night of Yom Kippur, the day of forgiveness of all sins and silences. My father roams about the rooms conversing and arguing with a God who is too foreign. Later on he brings us to a nearby river, whose dancing waters come from the distant and solemn cordilleras. He asks us to throw a rock in for each of our sins, but ultimately no one throws anything, no one repents, and we return home. My mother, who follows few rituals, lights the candles and says that it is time to remember the dead.

All the Yom Kippurs of my adolescence remind me of the ephemeral and intermittent nature of what I have lost in the exiles and voyages; they remind me of all that can never be ours again. Every Yom Kippur I think about the table in my maternal grandparents' home in Santiago, and I fill up with an inexplicable sadness, a sleepwalking muteness. We are alone and pray to an imaginary God. The reform temples of North America do not in the least remind me of the solemn majesty of the temples in my country. To me it seems as if the years only deepen the sense of loss, the feeling of always being absent in the distance and living amid the mist.

This Yom Kippur, I light the candles slowly. There are too many dead, and sometimes I feel I am living in a house of fear and memory, in a town filled with phantoms. Then I imagine myself returning to my father's boyhood home in Quillota, where his parents do not celebrate Yom Kippur, but know that it is the day of the dead, and I recognize myself as a young girl wedged between the thresholds, listening to that strange dialogue of silence and to my grandfather talking about the flames of Odessa when they fled, frightened like birds escaping terror. Only then do I realize that I should not throw any rocks.

At Yom Kippur I remember my father, who never went to temple or sought out congregations. He carries God in his tender heart.

## My Father's Memory

Astonished, and sunk within the silence of one who listens, I approach my father's memories and take refuge at the shore of his words. I listen to him diligently, eagerly, and as I write I invent him; I rearrange certain stories, disassemble others, and sort out his life, which is, above all else, mine as well. As I write about him, I feel his voice shifting in the silence with my own. I imagine him in that long-ago time when his thin hands marked the voyages.

In some way, by talking with my father, I have managed to talk about my own life and to tell how I was raised. Only through my father's story did I begin to understand about my own exile and now, in the most bewildering time of my life. surrounded by my two young children, I ask myself: Who was I? Who am I? Why do I write? To whom will I express my gratitude and my memory?

My father's memoirs respond to the wandering condition of most Jews, to always being from everywhere and nowhere, to writing in languages that were not theirs. Writing my father's memoirs is a way of confronting the faces of the departed and talking with dead relatives amid the shadows. It is also a way of struggling to legitimize histories.

The experience of exile, of coming from a line of haggard wanderers constantly recreating strange presences and looking at ourselves in mirrors to escape our own shadows, is the experience that shapes the disconnected memories of my father. But I also know that when I write about him, I am also writing the story of Jews lost in the most southern regions of the southern hemisphere, who prayed to the Virgen del Carmen, the patron saint of Santiago, and who had both crucifixes and Stars of David in their homes.

# A Gift

My father is short in stature. I like to watch him leave home and cross the immense tree-lined avenues, knowing that within a few hours he will return. He and my mother are the lights of my love, and I feel privileged to receive a piece of his life, of his sweet and sometimes silent voice, and to write of him. I have always given him poet's artifacts: fragile frogs, butterflies, and a box with a small ostrich egg. And now that I am older and have reached the middle of my life, I want to give him a book, this necklace of words to celebrate him.

*My father with his cousin, Gregorio Agosín, visiting Pablo Neruda's house on Isla Negra, 1985.*

*My father and me in Viña del Mar, celebrating my grandmother Josephine's ninetieth birthday.*

*My parents, my husband, me, and our son, Joseph, in Aix-en-Provence, in 1987.*

*My parents and me in Ogunquit, Maine, in the early 1990s.*

*My mother and father with my daughter, Sonia Helena, in Wellesley, 1993.*

*My father and Joseph in Ogunquit, 1993.*

*My parents in Wellesley on their fiftieth wedding anniversary, 19 July 1998.*

*My father, Moisés Agosín.*

# EPILOGUE

*My Father and I: Memories of Love*

## Faith

My father dries me off. Exhausted, we have returned from the seashore and another intense morning in the sun. His embrace is so familiar to me. He hugs me, dries my hair, and assures me that God does not exist, that he was invented in the rituals of the synagogues and temples. Most important of all, he tells me that we are Jews, who fight constantly with God as if this were our morning prayer.

I laugh and still don't know what to believe, but I pray a lot and praying soothes me and cures the sorrow in my soul. It seems as if it makes us more just and noble. I believe and don't believe. Ultimately, I choose to believe.

## Mist

At dawn, when the mist cut through the density of the morning, beyond the cool awakenings, my father would help us get dressed for school. To freshen us up, he washed our hair with lavender water. We shared breakfast in a sacred silence that helped us perceive even more that nearby and distant presence that was my father. This is why on the rare occasions when he spoke, his words seemed to be the source of a young and fast-flowing river.

We would arrive at school while the day was still immersed in shadow. The doorman greeted us with warm milk and we waited for the rest of the children, who arrive at eight. The children would play games and sing songs like, "Who stole the bread from the oven? "The Jewish dogs." I thought it strange that they only sang about Jewish and not Catholic dogs, and pondered the mysteries of canine religion.

Soon my father took us out of the public school and brought us to a school for Jewish children. There were also some Catholic children at the school, but they were so few in number that no one had to worry about them singing about dogs of any religious persuasion.

## Icons

When I turned six years old, one day as I was getting out of an immense claw-footed bathtub, my father said, "My child, God is an invention of the weak." This disturbed me greatly, so I decided to use all my energy praying to the Virgin Mary and to Saint Benito so that they would help me find lost objects. The Virgin Mary was very pretty, with her curls and tiny celestial eyes. She was a mother, like my own, and it was hard for me to fathom that people like my parents had killed her son.

## Doubts

When I finished reading *The Diary of Anne Frank,* I put it under my pillow so that the young Anne could be kept warm and fragrant in the darkness of my room between the starched sheets. I asked myself if there were really good people—a question that has accompanied me throughout childhood and into my adult life. Then I asked my father about the goodness of human beings, and he told me this story:

When his friend Haim escaped from the ghetto in Prague, he ran terrified through the streets of that so-familiar city. In desperation, he knocked on the door of a stranger and the stranger invited him in, in a random and unexpected gesture of solidarity between one being and another. However, as my father pointed out, at that moment, the man could just as easily have decided not to open the door. And it is in this mysterious ambiguity where the true spirit of altruism seems to lie.

## Soledad

My father taught me more through actions than through words. For example, he performed certain charitable acts without attaching much significance to them, as when he bought tee-shirts for the always-defeated soccer team of Quillota. All of these so-simple actions, like rings or alliances, make us believe that kindness lacks prerequisites.

In particular, I remember our Sunday visits with

Soledad. Soledad was a mentally retarded child, the daughter of a famous scientist in Chile who was a friend of my father. She was almost thirty years old when I met her and at times she seemed like a refugee, a displaced rag doll. My father took us to see Soledad every Sunday for almost ten years. There we played with her and kissed her, as if her fragile and very foreign life were a snail reposing in the lost obscurity of love. Soledad waited for us every Sunday. When we arrived, she gazed at us with her smoky eyes.

Soledad's own sister lived in a wheelchair, on the frontier of the dispossessed. From this chair she contemplated the intensity of time and a shaved life, and Soledad would caress her, repeating our examples of love, which we in turn had learned from my father, as if performing them with the least effort.

## Fate

I have been privileged to have my father in my life. He always urged me to explore creativity without limits and the eccentricities of innocence. He told me that human intelligence flourished when one kept it free from bonds and superfluous rules. My father is not an anarchist. He contemplates with sobriety and he likes to feel the essence of things as well as to investigate basic problems: How is creativity inherited? What does an enzyme signify? My father lets ideas flow. He explores with the peace of an intelligence that meditates and dreams.

## Mathematics

My father teaches me math and the sinister mysteries of subtraction, but I can't manage to take away or add. Then he explains numbers with flowers, seeds, and rocks. I am so mesmerized by the beauty of earthly things that I get distracted and never quite assimilate the fundamentals of arithmetic.

## Words

I learned to read while seated on my father's knees in that first and sacred moment when I began to sharpen my memory. My first book was a primer entitled *The Eye,* which was assigned in all Chilean elementary schools. Ever since that time I understood that all words lay buried in the fragile memory of the first gaze.

## Summers

My sister, my brother, and I play naked and freely on Chilean shores in the carefree heart of summer. Like an eccentric gentleman dressed in the garments of winter and all covered in moss and algae, my father reads science fiction and some Lorca poems. Suddenly his straw hat takes off madly in the wind, caught up in its own velocity, and we run after it. The hat swirls around like a white dress fleeing from unrequited love.

My father gives up the chase because he is accustomed

to losing many things. He doesn't change position, and continues reading his science fiction while the hat wanders and smiles between the pines and the wind, like an homage to time and to things lost and found.

## Dreams

My father asks me to tell him about my dreams, and I say that they are filled with earthquakes and merry-go-rounds, with lizards and restless mermaids. Then I request that we exchange dreams and that he share some stories with me. He tells me about a stone house buried in the Odessa woods and about a fire pursuing him through time. This is the home of his father, immersed in the most perfect and saddest of all winter desolations. Throughout his life, my grandfather had to flee in the wild and sinister night, in a night that was as mute as the barrenness of lonely women.

My father asks me to talk to him about my dreams, and I tell him that in my strange adulthood I am still on a merry-go-round. I also tell him that if I were to choose a favorite dream it would be the one about Quillota, where I would sleep in the house where he grew up and think of school days while gazing from the balconies and looking at the churches of the city.

## Secrets

I ask my father to tell me things and to approach the
first eclipse of memory. Sometimes I ask him to invent
stories and fables and to talk to me about nameless things
that bring him joy. He only tells me that he has been
and will continue to be for the rest of his life, a displaced
person, and that from the moment he speaks and pro-
nounces a word, those who hear him always want to
ascribe to him an origin, place, and class. When he tells
them his name, the curious calm down, knowing that
he is Jewish. They don't bother him about his origins
anymore. His name marks him with the tattoos of
intolerance. My father, too, perceives himself as a
Jewish man without a nation, a perpetual exile, which
is why he is called Moses.

I ask my father to talk to me about his memories and
his voice fades as if he were trying to weigh every one
of his words. He tells me that once upon a time there
was a boy named Moses who was saved from the
water and who, in a way, never left it.

## Belloto

My father has a dream, a wisp of breath, a gust filled
with desires that return him to Chile, to the reddish and
vanished earth. He wants to be near his parents in the
small and beautiful cemetery in Belloto, because there
everyone recognizes him. He wants to rest at last, to rest

his body in his country, where he will no longer be considered a foreigner and where he can rest next to his
dead. Here they will talk calmly and without haste, they
will speak softly and about love.

My father,
with a butterfly gait,
wavering between modernity
and antiquity,
distinguished
and humble,
is a gracious
gentleman,
prudent in his words,
perfidious with the arrogant,
noble and
winged with the poor,
respectful
of happiness.

CONTEMPORARY WOMEN'S FICTION
FROM AROUND THE WORLD
from The Feminist Press
at The City University of New York

*An Estate of Memory,* a novel by Ilona Karmel. $11.95 paper.

*Apples from the Desert: Selected Stories,* by Savyon Liebrecht. $19.95 hardcover.

*Bamboo Shoots After the Rain: Contemporary Stories by Women Writers of Taiwan.* $14.95 paper. $35.00 cloth.

*Cast Me Out If You Will,* stories and memoir by Lalithambika Antherjanam. $11.95 paper. $28.00 cloth.

*Changes: A Love Story,* a novel by Ama Ata Aidoo. $12.95 paper.

*Confessions of Madame Psyche,* a novel by Dorothy Bryant. $18.95 paper.

*The House of Memory: Stories by Jewish Women Writers of Latin America.* $15.95 paper. $37.00 cloth.

*Mulberry and Peach: Two Women of China,* a novel by Hualing Nieh. $12.95 paper.

*No Sweetness Here and Other Stories,* by Ama Ata Aidoo. $10.95 paper. $29.00 cloth.

*The Silent Duchess,* a novel by Dacia Maraini. $19.95 hardcover.

*The Slate of Life: More Contemporary Stories by Women Writers of India.* $12.95 paper. $35.00 cloth.

*The Tree and the Vine,* a novel by Dola de Jong. $9.95 paper, $27.95 cloth.

*Truth Tales: Contemporary Stories by Women Writers of India.* $12.95 paper. $35.00 cloth.

*Two Dreams: New and Selected Stories,* by Shirley Geok-lin Lim. $10.95 paper.

*What Did Miss Darrington See? An Anthology of Feminist Supernatural Fiction.* $14.95 paper.

*Women Writing in India: 600 B.C. to the Present. Volume I: 600 B.C. to the Early Twentieth Century.* $29.95 paper. *Volume II: The Twentieth Century.* $29.95 paper.

To receive a free catalog of The Feminist Press's 150 titles, call or write: The Feminist Press, Wingate Hall/City College, New York, NY 10031; phone: (212) 650-8966; fax: (212) 650-8893. Feminist Press books are available at bookstores or can be ordered directly. Send check or money order (in U.S. dollars drawn on a U.S. bank), adding $4.00 shipping and handling for the first book and $1.00 for each additional book, or call with your VISA, Mastercard, and American Express order. Prices subject to change.